CROWNED

IN

KENTUCKY

The Untold Story of Sovereignty, Junior
Alvarado, and Bill Mott's Epic Ride to Derby
Glory in 2025

By

Jake McDaniel

Table of Contents

Introduction – The Day the Crown Was Won

May 3, 2025. A warm, electric Saturday in Louisville, Kentucky. The sky above Churchill Downs shimmered with early summer sun, while a sea of hats, mint juleps, and anticipation swelled beneath it. It was Derby Day—the 151st running of the most iconic horse race in America— and the world was watching. Over 150,000 fans packed into the grandstands, and millions more tuned in from their living rooms, sports bars, mobile phones, and office screens around the globe. But no one—absolutely no one—could have predicted the moment that was about to unfold.

As the horses made their way to the starting gate, a palpable tension gripped the track. For weeks leading up to the Derby, all the buzz had circled around speedsters with flashy wins and celebrity ownerships. Pundits debated over favorites. Gamblers clutched betting slips. The crowd erupted into cheers, and then a hush, as the trumpet sounded its familiar, regal call.

Among the 20 contenders stood **Sovereignty**, a lean, muscular colt dressed in the royal blue silks of Godolphin—a global racing powerhouse still chasing its first Kentucky Derby win under its own colors. He wasn't the odds-on favorite. He wasn't even the biggest name on the board. But there was something about him that morning. Something calm. Something fierce. Something different.

Holding the reins was **Junior Alvarado**, a seasoned jockey who had spent nearly two decades chasing the Derby dream. Always respected but rarely center stage, Junior had tasted victory many times—but never here. Not at Churchill Downs. Not on the first Saturday in May. Yet, as he mounted Sovereignty that morning, a quiet confidence filled his eyes. This wasn't just another race. This was **his moment**.

Watching from the paddock rail was **Bill Mott**, a legend in the sport and a man who knew both glory and heartbreak. He had won the Derby once before—in 2019 with Country House—but that win came only after a disqualification. It was never the fairy tale ending most trainers dream of. This time, Mott wanted it clean. This time, he wanted it clear. This time, he wanted **redemption**.

The gates flew open at exactly 6:57 p.m.

A wall of muscle and fire surged forward, hooves pounding like thunder over the freshly raked dirt. The first furlongs were fast and furious. Sovereignty broke mid-pack—not too slow, not too aggressive. Alvarado kept him tucked along the rail, eyes focused, hands steady. Other horses pushed the pace early, some stumbling under pressure, some flying forward with reckless abandon. The lead changed hands twice before the first turn.

But Sovereignty was waiting.

Around the final bend, the crowd rose to their feet. The favorites were fading. The long shots were running out of gas. And through the dust and chaos, a blue flash emerged. It was Sovereignty—charging down the center, stride for stride, closing ground with every thunderous beat.

Alvarado gave a gentle nudge. The colt responded like a rocket.

The announcer's voice cracked with excitement.

"Here comes Sovereignty on the outside!"

The grandstands exploded. The cameras zoomed in. And in those final ten seconds—the world stood still. Every eye was glued to the blur of hooves and muscle and silk.

Sovereignty surged ahead in the last 50 yards. With three full strides left, he overtook the leader. With two strides, he sealed the win. And with one final, glorious stride, he crossed the finish line—first.

The crown was won.

Junior Alvarado stood tall in the stirrups, a smile breaking across his face like morning light. For a moment, he just soaked it in—the cheers, the flash of cameras, the rush of history. This was what he had dreamed of since he was a boy riding horses in Venezuela. This was for every year he'd come close. For every race he'd fought hard. For every doubt he had ever buried beneath his helmet.

And Bill Mott? He simply exhaled. Arms folded, eyes glassy, he gave a slow nod. He'd been here before—but never like this. No disqualifications. No technicalities. No asterisks. Just a perfect race, a brilliant horse, and a team that had earned every ounce of that victory.

The Churchill crowd roared as Sovereignty was led into the winner's circle. The blanket of red roses draped over his back like a royal cape. Cameras flashed. Reporters leaned in. And as Alvarado lifted the golden trophy, the chant began to rise from the crowd:

"Sovereignty! Sovereignty! Sovereignty!"

But this was more than just a victory. It was a story years in the making.

Sovereignty wasn't bred to be ordinary. He was the son of **Into Mischief**, one of the most successful sires of modern racing, and **Crowned**, a strong and underrated mare known for producing runners with heart. He was raised in Godolphin's lush paddocks and trained with precision and care.

Yet even with that legacy, he had to prove himself—race by race, stride by stride. The road to the Derby is never easy. Every contender faces setbacks. Every team must battle injuries, travel, pressure, and the ever-changing nature of horse racing. Sovereignty's journey was no different. But unlike others, he didn't just survive it—he **thrived**.

For Alvarado, this was more than a professional triumph. It was a personal victory. He had fought language barriers, cultural shifts, and tough competition from some of the best jockeys in the world. Over and over, he had been the guy who was "almost there." But not today. Today, he was **on top**.

And Bill Mott? Well, few trainers in history command the respect Mott does. With a career spanning decades, and wins at every level of the sport, he has always been known for his calm demeanor and classic training style. His 2019 Derby win was marred by controversy, as Maximum Security was disqualified and his horse, Country House, was elevated to first. That victory never felt complete. But this one? This one **was real**.

The moment Sovereignty crossed that line, something shifted—not just in the record books, but in the hearts of racing fans. It reminded people why they fall in love with this sport in the first place. It's not just about gambling or glamour. It's about **the story**—of the underdog, the unproven, the quiet confidence. It's about the connection between horse and human, the poetry in motion, the drama of 20 horses sprinting into history.

This win didn't just belong to Sovereignty, Alvarado, or Mott. It belonged to every groom who rose before sunrise. Every breeder who believed in bloodlines. Every fan who cried at the finish line. Every child in the infield watching a dream come alive.

As the sun set over Louisville and the champagne flowed, one thing was clear: the 151st Kentucky Derby would be remembered not just for the winner—but for **how** it was won. With heart. With harmony. With a horse named Sovereignty, a jockey named Junior Alvarado, and a trainer who proved that greatness doesn't fade—it deepens.

This book is the full story behind that crown. The roots, the rise, the race, and the legacy. You will meet the colt with a king's spirit. The rider with fire in his veins. And the horseman who stitched them together into champions.

This   is   **more**   **than**   a   **race.**
This is the journey to being **Crowned in Kentucky**.

Part I: The Making of a Champion

Every great champion starts with a dream—a hope in the heart of a breeder, a strategy in the mind of a trainer, and a fire burning in the soul of a young racehorse. But champions aren't just born. They are made. Forged through early mornings, hard lessons, careful planning, and the powerful belief that something extraordinary lies just around the bend. This is the story behind Sovereignty—the horse who stunned the world at the 2025 Kentucky Derby. This is how a colt became a king.

A Star Is Foaled

Sovereignty was born on a cool March morning in 2022 at one of the world's most prestigious breeding farms—Godolphin's American base in Kentucky. Owned by Sheikh Mohammed bin Rashid Al Maktoum, Godolphin has long been a towering name in global horse racing. With breeding operations stretching across continents, the organization is famous for producing fast, strong, and intelligent Thoroughbreds. But in all their victories, one prize had continued to elude them under their own silks—the Kentucky Derby.

Sovereignty's bloodline was promising from day one. His sire, **Into Mischief**, is one of the most successful stallions in North America. Known for passing down both speed and stamina, Into Mischief has sired numerous champions, including Derby contenders and Breeders' Cup winners. Sovereignty's dam, **Crowned**, may not have had a glittering racing career herself, but she was known for producing foals with heart, balance, and grit—qualities no champion can do without.

From the beginning, Sovereignty stood out. As a foal, he was curious, alert, and unusually calm for a youngster. While other colts would bolt at sudden noises or fight the lead rope, Sovereignty would pause, look, and learn. His handlers noted early that he had "an old soul." He watched the world with the quiet intensity of a horse that understood his place in it—he just hadn't taken it yet.

The Early Training Years

Training for Thoroughbreds starts early. By the time Sovereignty turned one, he had already learned the basics—how to lead, how to load into a trailer, how to wear a saddle, and how to walk and trot with balance. But it was when he turned two that the real work began.

He was sent to a training center in Florida, where the mornings begin before sunrise and the sound of hooves echoes through the mist. There, under the watchful eyes of seasoned horsemen, Sovereignty began his gallops, breezes, and gate training. His athleticism was evident from the start. But what impressed everyone even more was his mental sharpness. He didn't waste energy fighting the bit or bucking in rebellion. He listened. He focused. He improved.

Bill Mott, a Hall of Fame trainer known for his patient and intelligent approach, was assigned to guide Sovereignty's career. Mott had worked with legends like Cigar and had a deep understanding of how to bring out the best in a horse—not by pushing too hard too fast, but by building a solid foundation and letting the horse tell you when he's ready.

And Sovereignty? He told them he was ready.

The Road to the Derby

In 2024, as a 2-year-old, Sovereignty made his racing debut at Belmont Park. Though he didn't win that first race, he showed impressive closing speed and composure. It was clear this was no ordinary runner. In his next starts, Sovereignty began to shine—winning a maiden special weight, then taking down a Grade III stakes with ease.

As he matured into a 3-year-old in early 2025, all eyes turned toward the Derby trail—a series of important prep races that determine which horses qualify for the Kentucky Derby. Sovereignty ran in the **Holy Bull Stakes** at Gulfstream Park in January, finishing a strong second behind a pacesetter. Then came the **Fountain of Youth Stakes**, where he displayed a powerful burst of speed in the stretch to win by two lengths. But it was his performance in the **Florida Derby** that sealed his fate. Against a tough field, Sovereignty stalked the leaders with patience before unleashing a thrilling late charge to capture the win.

With enough qualifying points earned, Sovereignty punched his ticket to Louisville. He wasn't the betting favorite—that honor went to other flashy colts with more hype—but he had quietly earned the respect of trainers, jockeys, and bettors who knew what they were watching. He was strong. He was smart. He was dangerous.

The Team Behind the Horse

No champion rises alone. Behind Sovereignty was a dream team.

Bill Mott, with decades of experience, knew exactly how to prepare a horse for the Derby without burning him out. He scheduled breezes carefully, monitored the colt's weight and mental health, and kept him peeking at just the right time.

Junior Alvarado, the jockey, had built a strong partnership with Sovereignty. A native of Venezuela, Alvarado had spent years climbing the ladder of American racing. Though he had raced in multiple Triple Crown events before, the Derby win had always eluded him. But with Sovereignty, he felt something special—a horse who listened to him, trusted him, and responded with power.

The Godolphin team managed every detail. From nutrition and rest to travel and grooming, nothing was left to chance. The blue wave was coming to Louisville prepared, precise, and hungry for history.

Heart of a Champion

What truly makes a champion isn't just breeding or training—it's heart. And Sovereignty had it in abundance.

In his workouts at Churchill Downs leading up to the Derby, Sovereignty remained cool under pressure. He galloped with purpose. He handled the crowded backside with ease. Onlookers whispered that he looked "like he owned the place." He wasn't intimidated by the crowd, the cameras, or the chaos. He was there to do one thing—win.

And when the gates opened on May 3, 2025, that's exactly what he did.

But champions aren't just defined by how they win. They're remembered by what their victories mean. For Sovereignty, it was about more than roses. It was about fulfilling years of belief, effort, and quiet confidence. He didn't win with a flash. He won with class.

He became the first Godolphin horse to wear the Derby crown. He gave Junior Alvarado the ride of a lifetime. And he gave Bill Mott the kind of win every trainer dreams about—clean, commanding, and unforgettable.

Legacy in Motion

Though the 2025 Kentucky Derby was only the beginning of Sovereignty's journey, it will forever be the race that announced his greatness. The making of a champion isn't a single moment—it's a lifetime of small steps, each one building toward a burst of greatness that the world can finally see.

Sovereignty's story is a reminder that patience pays off. That the right horse, with the right people, at the right time, can rise from being one of many to standing alone at the finish line.

He wasn't the loudest. He wasn't the flashiest. But on the day it mattered most, **he was the best.**

And that is how champions are made.

The Birth of Sovereignty

A champion begins as a simple dream, a spark of potential waiting to be ignited. The story of Sovereignty, the sensational Kentucky Derby winner of 2025, is a tale not just of genetics, but of hope, patience, and a deep belief in something greater. His rise from a foal to a future star didn't happen overnight. It started with a foal born on a chilly morning in Kentucky, but the journey he embarked on—his path to greatness—was destined to make history.

The Foal That Was Born to Win

The morning of March 16, 2022, wasn't particularly remarkable in terms of weather or events—except for one thing: the birth of Sovereignty at **Godolphin's** renowned breeding farm in Lexington, Kentucky. Godolphin, led by the UAE's Sheikh Mohammed bin Rashid Al Maktoum, is one of the most prestigious breeding operations in the world, responsible for producing some of the best horses to ever race. So when Sovereignty entered the world, it wasn't just another birth. It was the beginning of what many would soon come to believe was something extraordinary.

Sovereignty's sire, **Into Mischief**, is a formidable presence in the world of horse racing. Known for producing exceptional speed and a competitive edge, Into Mischief's offspring have consistently made waves in high-level races. His influence is seen across the globe, with many of his progeny winning Grade 1 races and excelling in prestigious stakes events. When Sovereignty was born, he was, in many ways, already destined to carry the legacy of his father. However, it wasn't just his father's reputation that made Sovereignty special—it was his own qualities.

The dam of Sovereignty, **Crowned**, was a well-bred mare who herself didn't race to the heights of fame but was known for producing foals with one remarkable quality—heart. The combination of Into Mischief's speed and Crowned's tenacity made Sovereignty a blend of raw power and undeniable grit. As a foal, he showed early signs of greatness, but like any champion-to-be, he had to prove himself on the farm before he could prove himself on the track.

Early Days on the Farm

The farm where Sovereignty was born and raised was like many others in the heart of Kentucky's horse country—rolling hills, lush green fields, and the sound of hooves echoing across the land. But this farm wasn't just any farm. It was home to some of the most renowned bloodlines in racing, and it was here that Sovereignty would grow up, surrounded by greatness.

As a foal, Sovereignty had a quiet confidence about him. Unlike other foals that darted around with uncoordinated energy, Sovereignty moved with purpose. He was curious about the world around him, yet calm and observant, a trait that would define him as he matured. His handlers immediately noticed that there was something special in the way he carried himself, not just physically but mentally as well. This foal wasn't just going through the motions—he was learning, he was absorbing, and he was getting ready.

Even in those early days, there were whispers among the staff about his potential. "He's a thinker," one of the grooms said. "You can tell by the way he watches the other horses." Sovereignty wasn't the fastest at that age, nor the biggest. But he had something that couldn't be measured on a chart—he had presence. And presence, in the world of horse racing, is half the battle.

Signs of Promise: The Early Years

Sovereignty's growth in the early years of his life mirrored his potential. By the time he was weaned from his mother, Sovereignty had already started showing the characteristics that would later define him: strength, agility, and intelligence. He was a quick learner. He adapted easily to new situations and became known for his steady temperament. While most foals and yearlings might struggle with basic training, Sovereignty was always eager to please. Whether it was learning to stand for a blacksmith's hoof trim or getting used to the saddle, he was calm and cooperative.

As he grew older, Sovereignty's physical development became equally impressive. His stride was long, his body built with muscle and athleticism. His conformation was textbook: perfect balance between strength and flexibility. When he started galloping around the paddock, it was clear to his caretakers that his movement was effortless. He wasn't just running; he was gliding. His speed was natural, but it was his fluidity, his ability to turn and maneuver, that caught the eye of the trainers. This foal had raw talent, and the best part was that he seemed to know it.

What really set Sovereignty apart from the other young horses at Godolphin's farm, though, was his intelligence. He learned quickly not just the mechanics of training but the emotional side of it too. Horses are incredibly intuitive creatures. They can sense the energy of their surroundings and pick up on subtle cues from their handlers. Sovereignty was remarkably in tune with his environment. If his trainer spoke softly, Sovereignty would respond with calmness. If they increased their pace, Sovereignty would rise to meet the challenge, adjusting his speed with precision.

As Sovereignty approached the age of two, he had developed into a horse who was physically ready to train and emotionally prepared to race. His handlers began to take note of his ability to focus during workouts— something that's incredibly important for a racehorse. While other colts may have been distracted or overwhelmed by their first experiences on the track, Sovereignty remained composed, his eyes always locked on the finish line, even in training.

The Call to the Track: A New Chapter Begins

By the time Sovereignty turned two, it was clear that he was ready to take his talents from the farm to the racetrack. The decision was made: Sovereignty would enter training, and the world would soon discover whether the promise he had shown as a foal would translate into success on the track.

Bill Mott, the celebrated Hall of Fame trainer known for his measured approach to training, took the reins. Mott, who had seen the careers of many champions, quickly realized that Sovereignty was no ordinary horse. He wasn't just another contender. He was something special, a horse with a unique combination of power, speed, and intelligence.

Sovereignty's first training sessions were met with cautious optimism. Trainers and grooms alike observed his every movement. It wasn't long before they realized that Sovereignty wasn't just fast—he was smart, too. He handled the early workouts with confidence, and as he began to race in small, regional stakes, it became clear that he was a horse with a bright future ahead.

The excitement around Sovereignty began to build. While he wasn't an immediate frontrunner, the way he handled races caught the attention of the racing community. He didn't just win; he won with style, holding his position with remarkable control and speed. The world of horse racing had taken notice. Sovereignty wasn't just a foal with promise—he was a colt with a future, a future that might just include the greatest prize of all: the Kentucky Derby.

The Road to Greatness: Ready to Take on the World

From a foal to a future star, Sovereignty's rise was something of a fairy tale in the making. His early days on the farm were full of promise, and as he transitioned to life on the track, that promise began to take shape into reality. Sovereignty had all the ingredients for greatness: pedigree, physicality, temperament, and intelligence.

The journey of a racehorse is never simple. It's a journey filled with ups and downs, with challenges and setbacks. But the story of Sovereignty is one of unwavering potential—a promise that began with his birth and continues to evolve with every race he enters. His path to the Kentucky Derby was paved with the belief that he could do it all, and with each milestone he passed, he proved that belief was not misplaced.

From the moment he was born, Sovereignty was destined for greatness. But it was his early life, his time spent on the farm, that set the foundation for everything that was to come. The signs were clear: Sovereignty was not just another horse. He was a future champion. And as the racing world would soon learn, he was just getting started.

The Blue Silks of Godolphin: A Legacy of Racing Excellence

When you see the striking blue silks adorned by jockeys across some of the world's most prestigious racetracks, you are not just witnessing a piece of fabric in motion; you are witnessing the result of a carefully cultivated legacy, one that spans continents and decades. These iconic blue silks belong to **Godolphin**, the internationally renowned thoroughbred racing and breeding operation based in Dubai, United Arab Emirates. Its history, its breeding philosophy, and its unwavering pursuit of excellence have shaped the world of racing in ways few organizations ever could.

From the deserts of the UAE to the verdant tracks of America, the blue silks of Godolphin represent a force of nature in the world of horse racing—a team that continues to make waves with every race it enters. But this success is not by accident. Behind Godolphin's impressive list of achievements lies a strategic vision that began decades ago with a singular goal: to conquer the world's most iconic races and forever leave its mark on the sport.

The Birth of Godolphin: A Vision Realized

The story of Godolphin begins with its founder, **Sheikh Mohammed bin Rashid Al Maktoum**, the ruler of Dubai and one of the most influential figures in the world of horse racing. Sheikh Mohammed's passion for horses was evident from an early age, and his dream was always to elevate the sport of horse racing to new heights. In 1992, he founded Godolphin with the aim of creating a breeding operation that would stand on the same level as the world's best. This was a bold vision, especially considering the immense competition from established operations in places like Europe and the United States.

At the heart of Sheikh Mohammed's vision was a single guiding principle: **quality over quantity**. He understood that to be truly successful, a stable would need not just a quantity of horses but horses that embodied perfection in every regard: bloodlines, physicality, temperament, and racing pedigree. Godolphin's early success was based on this very principle, and it was soon clear that Sheikh Mohammed's operation was something different. Unlike other breeding operations, Godolphin combined its impeccable breeding practices with a rigorous, race-focused strategy, which ultimately allowed them to turn out champions, not just in the UAE, but on racetracks across the world.

But for all of Godolphin's successes on home turf, the true test of the operation's reach would come when they set their sights on the most coveted races on earth, particularly in America. For all the global recognition Godolphin earned, there was one prize that stood out among the rest: the **Kentucky Derby**, America's most iconic and prestigious horse race.

Godolphin's Quest for the Kentucky Derby

For a stable with such an extensive and successful international presence, the Kentucky Derby—held annually at Churchill Downs in Louisville, Kentucky—was a race that was almost mythically elusive. While Godolphin had seen success in Europe, winning major races like the **Prix de l'Arc de Triomphe** and **Royal Ascot**, America's top race had yet to be conquered. This was a problem Godolphin set out to fix.

The Kentucky Derby, with its rich history and immense prestige, has long been considered the holy grail of horse racing. Winning the Derby is not just about claiming a prize; it is about cementing one's legacy in the annals of racing history. Despite its global success, Godolphin had struggled to win the race for many years, with its horses often coming close, but falling just short. Nevertheless, the determination to win remain unshaken, and with each year, the blue silks seemed to come closer to claiming the crown.

The challenge in winning the Derby was no small feat. The race attracts the best horses from all over the world, and each year, it features fresh contenders eager to prove themselves. However, Godolphin's tenacity and persistence ultimately paid off. Their first true breakthrough came in 2025 with the victory of **Sovereignty**, an impressive colt who became the symbol of Godolphin's commitment to not just race, but to dominate. Sovereignty's win marked a pivotal moment in the organization's quest for the Derby, turning a dream into reality.

Yet, this victory was only a part of a larger plan. Godolphin's approach to the Derby wasn't about being a one-hit wonder—it was part of a larger blueprint to make their mark on American racing. Sovereignty's win set the stage for more successes, and it solidified the organization's commitment to excellence in the sport.

The Blue Silks: An International Presence

While the goal of winning the Kentucky Derby has been a major focus for Godolphin, the operation's influence stretches far beyond American soil. Across Europe, Asia, and Australia, the blue silks have come to represent power, grace, and excellence in the world of horse racing. In the UK, Godolphin horses regularly dominate the top-tier races at **Royal Ascot And** the **Epsom Derby**. Their European influence cannot be overstated, with horses consistently finishing in the top positions of major international races.

One of the key factors behind Godolphin's success is its ability to tap into the best breeding programs worldwide. Unlike many other stables that focus exclusively on the racing side of things, Godolphin's breeding philosophy places just as much importance on producing the next generation of winners. Through a combination of strategically chosen bloodlines, extensive scouting, and collaboration with top breeders across the world, Godolphin has built one of the most sophisticated breeding operations in existence.

But breeding is only half the equation. Godolphin has also invested heavily in training, employing some of the most experienced and successful trainers in the world. This combination of top-tier breeding and expert training has led to a consistent track record of success, with Godolphin horses winning some of the world's most prestigious races across multiple continents.

The Godolphin Philosophy: Breeding for the Future

Godolphin's breeding philosophy is one that places a premium on quality, but it also looks towards the future. It is a philosophy rooted in long-term success rather than quick wins. Sheikh Mohammed has always emphasized that the goal isn't just to win today's races, but to build a legacy that will last for generations.

The operation focuses heavily on bloodlines, ensuring that every mare and stallion used for breeding has a proven history of excellence. But beyond genetics, Godolphin looks for other attributes in its horses: resilience, intelligence, and the ability to learn and adapt. These qualities are crucial for a horse that will be racing at the highest level, where the competition is fierce and the stakes are high. This careful selection process, combined with expert training and a state-of-the-art breeding operation, allows Godolphin to stay ahead of the curve and produce horses that excel in major races worldwide.

Another key aspect of Godolphin's philosophy is its commitment to supporting and nurturing the horses long after they've raced. The organization is known for its high standards of care, ensuring that each horse is given the best possible environment in which to thrive. This commitment to well-being allows Godolphin to not only produce top-tier athletes but also to ensure their horses have long, healthy careers.

The Legacy Continues: Godolphin's Future in Racing

As Godolphin moves forward, the future looks incredibly bright. The organization has not only succeeded in winning some of the world's biggest races but has also built an unmatched legacy in global horse racing. Their impact is felt across every major racetrack, and with the win of Sovereignty at the Kentucky Derby, the blue silks have truly cemented their place in the sport's history.

Godolphin's international influence continues to grow, with the organization expanding its presence in emerging racing markets like Asia and the Middle East. As Sheikh Mohammed's vision continues to unfold, there's no doubt that Godolphin will continue to dominate on the global stage.

The story of Godolphin is one of passion, perseverance, and a constant drive for excellence. From its humble beginnings to its current status as one of the most successful racing operations in the world, the blue silks of Godolphin have come to represent the very best of horse racing—an unyielding commitment to success, a legacy of champions, and a relentless pursuit of greatness. The future of Godolphin is as bright as ever, and with each passing race, the world will continue to watch in awe as the blue silks charge toward new victories and new milestones.

Into Mischief's Legacy: The DNA Behind a Derby Champion

In the world of thoroughbred horse racing, few names carry as much weight as **Into Mischief**. Known for his fierce racing prowess and incredible influence as a sire, Into Mischief's legacy is one that stretches far beyond his own racing days. His name is synonymous with success, and his DNA has passed on to some of the greatest racehorses of the modern era. One such product of his legacy is **Sovereignty**, a horse whose dominance in the Derby speaks volumes about Into Mischief's remarkable genetic impact.

To understand Sovereignty's success on the racetrack, one must first take a closer look at the stallion whose genetic traits helped shape this champion. **Into Mischief** wasn't just a powerful horse in his prime; his impact as a sire is felt today in the form of fast, resilient, and elite racehorses. Let's explore Into Mischief's legacy and how his genes helped create the Derby champion, Sovereignty, who has gone on to carve his own path in racing history.

Into Mischief: The Stallion Who Changed the Game

Born in 2005, Into Mischief was a standout racehorse whose performances on the track earned him a respected place in the racing community. With an impressive pedigree himself, his racing career set the stage for his later role as a sire. During his time racing, Into Mischief proved to be one of the most competitive sprinters, winning races such as the **Hollywood Prevue Stakes** and finishing strong in many other major events. However, it was his transition from the racetrack to the breeding shed where he truly began to make his mark.

Sired by **Harlan's Holiday**—a well-known figure in the racing world—Into Mischief possessed the perfect combination of speed, stamina, and competitive spirit. These traits were passed on to his offspring, and his progeny began to dominate in both sprint and route races. His DNA became synonymous with athleticism, grit, and determination—qualities that would prove invaluable in shaping champions like Sovereignty.

Mischief's transition to the breeding shed came in 2009, and it wasn't long before his offspring began to show incredible promise. His horses were not just quick; they were smart, resilient, and often able to perform under the toughest conditions. This made him a favorite among breeders looking to produce competitive racehorses with the pedigree and temperament to excel on big stages.

The Sire of Champions: A Breeding Phenomenon

Since his arrival in the breeding shed, Into Mischief has become one of the most prolific and successful sires in modern racing. His breeding record speaks for itself. He has produced a staggering number of grade 1 winners, many of whom have gone on to win some of the most prestigious races around the world. His progeny includes **Authentic**, the 2020 Kentucky Derby winner, **Vekoma**, the 2019 Blue Grass Stakes winner, and **Goldencents**, another multiple Grade 1 winner.

But what makes Into Mischief's breeding record so exceptional isn't just the number of winners, but the consistency of the success. Year after year, his horses perform at the highest levels, competing in and winning some of the most competitive races globally. This remarkable success in producing world-class horses made him an extremely valuable stallion and cemented his place as one of the dominant figures in thoroughbred breeding.

Into Mischief's legacy as a sire is also marked by the versatility of his offspring. His bloodline has produced winners in a wide range of races—ranging from sprints to longer-distance events. His ability to sire horses that can perform across multiple disciplines is a testament to the versatility and depth of his genetic influence. This versatility was crucial for horses like Sovereignty, who had to excel in one of the most grueling races in the world—the Kentucky Derby.

Sovereignty: The Derby Champion Shaped by Into Mischief's DNA

Sovereignty's rise to prominence in the world of thoroughbred racing is no accident. While the colt has undoubtedly earned his place among the stars through his own talent and determination, his success is deeply intertwined with the incredible genetic foundation laid down by his sire, Into Mischief. Sovereignty's victory in the **Kentucky Derby** was a defining moment for both the horse and the Godolphin operation, and it was in many ways the culmination of a long-standing partnership between world-class breeding and racing strategy.

Sovereignty inherited much of his sire's athleticism and speed. Mischief's influence is immediately apparent in Sovereignty's sprinting prowess. Like his sire, Sovereignty is a powerful and fast runner, able to explode out of the gate and maintain top speeds for long stretches. Mischief's legacy of competitive fire is visible in every stride Sovereignty takes, especially when it matters most—on the world's biggest stage.

Moreover, Sovereignty's ability to maintain composure in high-pressure situations, such as the Kentucky Derby, is another trait directly linked to his father's influence. Mischief's offspring are known for their ability to race under pressure, and Sovereignty is no exception. This mental resilience, combined with physical speed, made Sovereignty a formidable competitor in the Derby, where maintaining composure and executing strategy under pressure is key.

But it isn't just speed and resilience that Sovereignty gained from Into Mischief's DNA—it's also a strong will to win. Into Mischief was known for his competitive nature on the track, and that drive is something he passed on to his offspring. Sovereignty's relentless push to the front of the pack in the Derby was a direct reflection of this characteristic, a trait that made him a standout on one of racing's biggest stages.

Into Mischief's Genetic Blueprint: Speed, Stamina, and Intelligence

When it comes to breeding thoroughbreds, the combination of speed, stamina, and intelligence is critical. Into Mischief's success as a sire is largely due to his ability to transmit these qualities to his progeny. His DNA is finely tuned to produce horses that not only possess raw speed but also the stamina to carry that speed over longer distances— an essential feature for a horse vying for major titles like the Kentucky Derby.

Sovereignty benefited greatly from this genetic blueprint. His speed on the track was evident early in his career, as he quickly established himself as a formidable force in sprints and longer races. However, the endurance and focus required to win the Derby are just as important, and Sovereignty was able to demonstrate both in abundance. Thanks to the influence of Into Mischief's genes, Sovereignty had the stamina to go the distance and the intellect to make the right moves at the right time.

Mischief's progeny have demonstrated time and time again that his genes are capable of producing horses with not only the raw talent to compete at the highest levels but also the mental toughness to thrive under intense pressure. This dual combination of physical ability and mental acuity is precisely what makes horses like Sovereignty stand out and continue to win major races across the globe.

A Legacy that Will Last for Generations

The success of Into Mischief is not just about the horses he sired during his own career. His legacy extends far beyond his own racing days, as he continues to be one of the most sought-after stallions in the world. His offspring continue to dominate the racetracks, year after year, proving that his influence is not just a flash in the pan—it is a lasting and transformative force in the world of thoroughbred racing.

With each new generation of horses sired by Into Mischief, his impact grows stronger. His bloodline has become synonymous with excellence, and it is clear that the future of racing will continue to feel the influence of this exceptional stallion for many years to come. Sovereignty's victory in the Kentucky Derby is a shining example of the kind of racehorse that Into Mischief produces—a champion who is fast, smart, and resilient.

As the world watches the next chapter in Sovereignty's career unfold, there is little doubt that his success is inextricably linked to the incredible legacy of his sire, Into Mischief. The blueprint for greatness has already been set, and as long as his genes continue to be passed down, the future of thoroughbred racing will remain bright. Into Mischief's legacy is one that will be remembered not just for the champions he produced, but for the enduring impact he had on the sport of horse racing as a whole.

Crowned: A Mare's Silent Power

In the world of thoroughbred racing, it is often easy to focus on the stallions—the powerful, high-profile racehorses whose genetic contributions to the sport are celebrated across the globe. Yet, behind every successful racehorse, there is often an equally powerful figure working quietly in the background—the mare. While the stallion's prowess on the track garners much attention, it is the mare who carries the promise of greatness from the beginning. This is especially true when we look at **Sovereignty**, the star Derby winner, and the unspoken influence of his dam, **Crowned**.

In a world where male influence often dominates the spotlight, Crowned stands as a reminder of the quiet but powerful role mares play in shaping champions. **Crowned**, though less celebrated in public recognition than her offspring, carries a legacy of resilience, grace, and strength that flows through her progeny—none more prominently than in Sovereignty, who carries his dam's legacy to the highest stage in racing.

This essay will explore Crowned's silent power, examining how mares like her influence thoroughbred racing in ways that are often underappreciated, and how Crowned's genetic contributions have shaped Sovereignty into the racehorse he is today.

The Importance of the Dam in Thoroughbred Racing

In the world of thoroughbred breeding, much of the focus is placed on the sire—the stallion whose performance on the track and genetic gifts shape the potential of the next generation. Yet, the importance of the dam cannot be overstated. The dam's influence on the offspring goes far beyond simply carrying the foal; she imparts crucial traits such as temperament, durability, and stamina. While a stallion like **Into Mischief** may provide speed, power, and competitive drive, it is the dam who often shapes the horse's heart and mind, influencing its ability to withstand the pressures of racing.

In racing, stamina and mental resilience are just as important as speed, and these qualities are often passed down from the dam. A mare like Crowned has a quiet but potent influence over her offspring's ability to handle the intense demands of the racetrack. Her genetics shape how Sovereignty reacts to pressure, how he manages the stress of competition, and how he performs under the most grueling conditions.

Crowned's maternal line is more than just a genetic foundation—she represents the values that make champions in the sport. Her contribution to Sovereignty's success is not immediately obvious; it's the quiet strength in his every stride, the unshakable determination in the heat of competition, and the mental focus that enables him to thrive under the spotlight. These are the gifts Crowned passed on to Sovereignty.

Crowned's Pedigree: A Legacy of Strength and Grace

To understand the power that Crowned brought to her offspring, we must look at her own pedigree. Crowned was not just any mare; she descended from a line of thoroughbreds known for their durability, intelligence, and ability to perform at the highest levels. Her lineage traces back to some of the most successful and influential horses in racing history, contributing to the mental and physical qualities that would later manifest in Sovereignty.

Her own performances on the track may not have been as widely known as the stars of her generation, but this does not diminish her influence. Like many successful dams, Crowned's true power lies not in her race record, but in her ability to transmit excellence to her progeny. She was known for passing on a calm demeanor, a strong will to win, and a tenacity that often goes unnoticed but is crucial to a horse's success.

Crowned's family history is a testament to the strength of her maternal line. The mares in her lineage had a consistent record of producing racehorses who thrived under pressure, performing consistently in high-stakes races. This deep-rooted history of excellence is something that Sovereignty inherited, as Crowned passed on the genetic traits that made him a standout in the Kentucky Derby.

Maternal Influence: The Hidden Power Behind Sovereignty's Success

When Sovereignty crossed the finish line to claim victory in the **Kentucky Derby**, it was a moment that captured the hearts of racing fans around the world. His success was not only a tribute to his sire, **Into Mischief**, but also to his dam, **Crowned**, whose quiet strength flowed through every stride. While Sovereignty's sire contributed the raw speed and competitive nature needed for the race, it was Crowned who added the mental fortitude, the ability to maintain focus in a crowded field, and the stamina to go the distance.

Crowned's influence is evident in Sovereignty's ability to handle pressure—one of the most challenging aspects of racing. The Kentucky Derby is often described as one of the most intense races, where the horses are pushed to their physical and mental limits. It is during these moments that a horse's ability to stay composed, calm, and focused becomes crucial. Sovereignty's unwavering concentration and stamina throughout the race are qualities that stem directly from Crowned's influence. This hidden power, inherited through the maternal line, gave Sovereignty the tools he needed to succeed on the grandest stage.

The Quiet Strength of the Dam

While stallions like Into Mischief are celebrated for their direct impact on the racehorse's physical attributes, the dam's role is often overshadowed by this spotlight. However, the quiet strength of mares like Crowned is irreplaceable. The dam's role in thoroughbred racing is not always in the public eye, but it is felt deeply in the success of the horse. It is the dam who shapes the heart and soul of the horse—the inner strength, the focus, and the drive that push a horse to greatness.

Crowned's influence extends beyond genetics—it is a story of maternal dedication and strength. As any breeder or trainer will attest, mares like Crowned are essential to the success of racing. The maternal line is the backbone of a horse's emotional and physical development, and Crowned provided Sovereignty with the resilience and stamina needed to thrive at the highest levels of competition. It is this quiet power that enables Sovereignty to remain competitive and calm when facing the challenges of the racetrack.

The Value of the Maternal Line in Modern Racing

In modern thoroughbred racing, the maternal line is beginning to receive the recognition it deserves. As breeding techniques continue to evolve and more is understood about genetics, it becomes increasingly clear that the dam's influence is just as important as the sire's. This shift in perspective has led to a greater appreciation of mares like Crowned, whose contribution to the sport extends far beyond what meets the eye.

In the case of Sovereignty, Crowned's influence cannot be overstated. It was her strength and resilience that allowed him to stand tall on the starting line of the Kentucky Derby, and it is her silent power that continues to fuel his success as he races through his career. This shift in focus toward recognizing the dam's role is essential for the future of the sport, ensuring that mares like Crowned are given the credit they deserve.

The Continuing Influence of Crowned's Line

As Sovereignty continues to race and make a name for himself in the sport, the legacy of Crowned lives on. The quiet strength she imparted to him will resonate in future generations of thoroughbreds, ensuring that her influence continues to shape the sport for years to come. Sovereignty's achievements on the racetrack are not just a tribute to his sire, but to Crowned, whose maternal influence provided him with the tools to become a champion.

The story of Crowned is a reminder that in racing, as in life, sometimes the quietest voices are the most powerful. While the stallions may command attention for their speed and strength, it is the mares who lay the foundation for greatness. Through Crowned unwavering strength, Sovereignty has become a living testament to the silent, yet undeniable, power of the maternal line in thoroughbred racing.

Part II: The Horsemen Behind the Horse

In the dazzling world of thoroughbred racing, the limelight is often reserved for the horses—their swift strides, the triumphs, the heart-stopping finishes, and the roar of the crowd. But behind every great horse, there are men and women whose skill, dedication, and knowledge shape the very essence of that champion. These are the **horsemen behind the horse**, the trainers, jockeys, grooms, and breeders whose influence is just as crucial as the horse's natural talent.

While the horses themselves may receive all the glory, it is the horsemen who mold them into the racehorses capable of achieving greatness. This essay delves deep into the world of the horsemen who guide these magnificent creatures, focusing on their roles, the relationships they build with their horses, and how they elevate the sport of racing. It's a story of teamwork, trust, and unwavering dedication that extends far beyond the finish line.

The Trainer: The Architect of a Champion

The role of the **trainer** is perhaps the most visible and influential in the racing world. A trainer is not only responsible for shaping a horse's physical condition but also for crafting a strategy that allows the horse to compete at the highest levels. They are the ones who decide when the horse should rest, when to push it to its limits, and how to nurture its potential. The bond between trainer and horse is a unique one, built on trust and understanding.

Take **Sovereignty**, for instance—a horse that has reached the pinnacle of racing success, thanks in large part to the expertise of his trainer. Trainers work with racehorses from a young age, guiding them through the complexities of race training and teaching them how to harness their instincts in ways that optimize performance. The daily routine of training, whether on the track, in the stables, or in the gym, is crucial for a horse's development.

In the case of Sovereignty, his trainer's influence is deeply felt. The decisions made on his training regimen, the races he runs, and how he handles different conditions are all shaped by the trainer's vision. The trainer also plays a pivotal role in the horse's mental conditioning. Racehorses need more than just physical stamina—they need mental toughness to handle the noise, the crowds, and the pressure of competition. Trainers like Sovereignty's help instill this resilience, ensuring that the horse is ready to face whatever challenges come its way.

The Jockey: The Silent Partner in Victory

The **jockey** is the individual who actually guides the horse during the race, and while they may be less visible during training, their role in the final performance is critical. A jockey's ability to communicate with the horse through subtle cues, their timing, and their tactical awareness can be the difference between victory and defeat.

A great jockey is often described as having an innate connection with their horse—a sixth sense that allows them to anticipate the horse's movements, adjust mid-race, and strategically position themselves for the best possible outcome. This partnership requires an understanding built over time and, often, years of riding together. While a horse may have natural speed and agility, it is the jockey who ensures those attributes are fully realized during the race.

For Sovereignty, having the right jockey was instrumental in his victory. The jockey's intimate knowledge of the horse's behavior, strengths, and weaknesses was vital. A great jockey knows how to keep a horse calm in the chaos of a race, how to time a push for speed perfectly, and how to guide the horse through tight spots. This silent partnership between horse and jockey is often underestimated, but without it, even the best horses would not achieve their full potential.

The Groom: The Unsung Hero

Behind every winning horse, there is also an unsung hero— the **groom**. The groom is the one who spends the most time with the horse, taking care of its daily needs, ensuring its health, and maintaining its well-being. From feeding and bathing to brushing and ensuring the horse is comfortable, the groom's role is vital in keeping the horse in top condition.

It is the groom who ensures that the horse is ready for training and the race ahead. Their attention to detail— whether it's the cleanliness of the stable, the condition of the hooves, or the health of the coat—plays a crucial role in the horse's overall performance. The groom's familiarity with the horse also allows them to spot any potential issues or signs of fatigue that could hinder the horse's ability to race. Often working behind the scenes, grooms provide the foundation on which everything else is built.

Grooms develop an intimate connection with the horses they care for, and that relationship is based on trust. Horses are creatures of habit, and the familiarity of a groom's presence can calm a horse and keep it comfortable. The long hours spent with the horse, the quiet moments of care, and the routine of the stable are crucial for ensuring the horse is ready for competition.

The Breeder: Crafting the Legacy

The **breeder** is the person who lays the foundation for the entire career of a racehorse. From choosing the right parents, to overseeing the foaling process, and ensuring the young horse has the necessary care and environment to grow, the breeder's role is essential to producing successful horses. It is the breeder who ensures that the bloodlines are strong, and that the horse has the best chance to develop the traits needed for success in racing.

For Sovereignty, his pedigree and the careful selection of his parents contributed to his natural talents. Breeders play a long-term role, making decisions that will affect the horse's future without always being present at the moment of glory. The early years of a horse's life are critical, and breeders ensure that these years are spent in the best conditions possible. They also provide the initial training and nurturing that helps young horses develop the skills they need to succeed.

A good breeder understands the traits that are desirable in a racing horse—speed, stamina, intelligence—and seeks to produce horses that embody those qualities. Their work is a blend of science and intuition, involving careful research and an understanding of genetics, as well as a deep love for the sport.

The Team: A Collective Effort

The success of a racehorse is not the result of one person's work; it is a team effort. The trainer, jockey, groom, and breeder all play crucial roles in the horse's journey to victory. Each individual brings their expertise, dedication, and passion to the table, working together to create a champion. Their efforts may be behind the scenes, but their contributions are just as vital as the horse's talent.

This collective effort is what allows a horse like Sovereignty to reach the peak of his career. The teamwork between horse and horsemen enables the horse to achieve his full potential. It is the careful coordination of all these roles that makes racing such a unique and exhilarating sport.

The Legacy of the Horsemen

The horsemen behind the horse are more than just caretakers—they are partners in the journey, helping shape a horse's destiny. In Sovereignty's case, the trainer, jockey, groom, and breeder all contributed to his success, but they also created a legacy that extends beyond just one horse. They helped build the foundation for future horses, passing down knowledge, techniques, and practices that continue to influence the sport.

Racing is a sport built on history, tradition, and passion, and the horsemen who dedicate their lives to it are the unsung heroes who help keep that legacy alive. It is through their expertise, their commitment, and their love for the animals that the sport of thoroughbred racing continues to thrive, generation after generation.

In conclusion, while the horse may be the star of the show, it is the horsemen who deserve much of the credit for any victory. The trainer, jockey, groom, and breeder are the unsung heroes who mold the horse into a champion. Their teamwork, their dedication, and their intimate knowledge of the horse are what make the sport of racing so exciting and awe-inspiring. The horsemen behind the horse are the true architects of success, and without them, even the greatest horses would not reach their full potential.

Junior Alvarado: The Long Road to Churchill Downs

In the world of horse racing, the journey to becoming a Derby-winning jockey is often filled with immense challenges, tough decisions, and a series of personal and professional hurdles that test both heart and will. Few embody this story of perseverance and triumph like Junior Alvarado. From the racetracks of Venezuela to standing atop the winner's circle at the Kentucky Derby, Alvarado's journey is a testament to grit, dedication, and the unwavering belief in the dream of one day riding in the most prestigious race in the world. This is the story of how Junior Alvarado defied the odds and overcame countless obstacles to claim his place in history at Churchill Downs.

Early Beginnings: The Roots of a Dream

Born in the small city of Maracaibo, Venezuela, in 1988, Juan "Junior" Alvarado's love for horses began at a young age. Raised in a country where horse racing holds deep cultural roots, Alvarado was surrounded by the sport from his earliest days. His family wasn't wealthy, but they had a strong connection to the racing world. His uncle, who worked as a trainer, gave Junior his first taste of the racetrack. It didn't take long for the young boy to fall in love with the excitement, beauty, and power of thoroughbred racing.

In Venezuela, Alvarado watched as many young jockeys learned the art of racing, often starting as young as 14 or 15. Inspired by the legends he saw on the track, Junior decided he wanted to pursue a career as a jockey. His dream wasn't just about fame or the potential for riches—it was about the love of horses and the rush of riding in the heat of competition. However, the road to success was not going to be easy.

At just 14 years old, Alvarado left home to begin his formal training as a jockey in Venezuela. Like many young riders, he faced the harsh realities of the sport. The training was intense, demanding physical and mental stamina that was beyond what most young adolescents were prepared for. For years, Alvarado raced at smaller tracks in Venezuela, gaining experience and refining his skills. However, success didn't come overnight. He faced a lot of struggles, competing against much more seasoned riders, many of whom were much older and more established in the industry.

A Leap of Faith: The Move to America

Alvarado's big break came when he made the decision to leave Venezuela for the United States—a move that would mark the beginning of his real journey to the top of the sport. At the age of 20, Alvarado arrived in the United States with only a small amount of money in his pocket and a burning desire to make a name for himself. He settled in New York, hoping that the competitive and bustling racing scene would provide the opportunity he needed to prove himself.

The transition wasn't easy. Racing in America is a far cry from racing in Venezuela. The tracks are bigger, the competition is fiercer, and the expectations are higher. For Junior, it was a culture shock. He didn't speak much English, and he had to adapt quickly to a whole new way of life. But what he lacked in resources and familiarity, he made up for with sheer determination. Junior Alvarado quickly proved that he was a force to be reckoned with.

His first years in the U.S. were filled with setbacks. He struggled to land significant rides, and when he did, they didn't always go as planned. The competition for rides was fierce, with jockeys who had been racing for decades dominating the circuits. But Alvarado didn't give up. He worked tirelessly to improve his skills, watching and learning from the more experienced jockeys and trainers around him. He built relationships with owners and trainers, all while trying to stay true to his craft.

Breaking Through: Building Momentum

It wasn't long before Alvarado began to earn more respect in the American racing scene. His breakthrough moment came in 2010 when he started winning consistently at Aqueduct Racetrack in New York. He developed a reputation for his calm, cool demeanor and his strategic approach to racing, which helped him secure more high-profile rides. However, he knew that to truly make a name for himself, he would need to take his talents to some of the most important racetracks in the country. His rise to prominence continued through 2011 and 2012 as he began riding at the famed Saratoga Race Course and Belmont Park.

Alvarado's dedication and persistence began to pay off. He started to win big races, and his reputation as one of the best jockeys in the country started to grow. But even with these wins, he knew that he had not yet reached the pinnacle of American horse racing—the Kentucky Derby.

The Kentucky Derby Dream

The Kentucky Derby is the race every jockey dreams of, and for Junior Alvarado, the dream was no different. The journey to Churchill Downs is often long, with many jockeys spending years working toward the one race that can define their careers. For Alvarado, the Derby was a distant but highly motivating goal. In 2019, after years of hard work and relentless dedication, Alvarado was finally able to ride in the Kentucky Derby aboard the horse "Maximum Security." While Maximum Security was disqualified after crossing the finish line first, the experience was a major milestone in Alvarado's career, providing him with invaluable knowledge of the Derby atmosphere and preparation.

In 2025, after years of narrowly missing out on the big win, Junior Alvarado would finally get the chance to taste victory in the Kentucky Derby. This time, his ride aboard the talented Sovereignty would prove to be the breakthrough he had been waiting for. As the horses lined up on the starting gate and the crowd roared in anticipation, Alvarado's years of dedication, his unyielding spirit, and his deep understanding of the sport would lead him to one of the most monumental wins of his career.

The Victory: A Dream Realized

On May 3, 2025, Junior Alvarado made history as he guided Sovereignty to victory in the 151st Kentucky Derby. The day was filled with drama, excitement, and emotion, but for Alvarado, it was the culmination of everything he had worked for. As Sovereignty crossed the finish line, the long road that began in Venezuela and took him through the toughest challenges of American racing had finally led him to the pinnacle of the sport.

Alvarado's victory was not only a personal triumph but also a win for the entire racing community. It was a reminder that no dream is too big, and no challenge is too great to overcome. His story is one of resilience, passion, and the power of never giving up, no matter how many times life or the sport might knock you down.

The Legacy

Junior Alvarado's journey is far from over. The Kentucky Derby win marked a new chapter in his life, one that will be remembered by fans of horse racing for years to come. But more than just a Derby victory, Alvarado's story is a beacon of hope for anyone who dares to chase their dreams, no matter where they come from or how difficult the path may seem. From his humble beginnings in Venezuela to the winner's circle at Churchill Downs, Alvarado's legacy is one of perseverance and triumph. It's a legacy that will inspire future generations of jockeys, athletes, and dreamers alike to keep fighting, to keep believing, and to keep riding toward their goals.

Bill Mott: The Master Trainer Returns

In the world of horse racing, few names carry as much respect and admiration as Bill Mott. A legendary figure in the sport, Mott's career has been built on decades of expertise, dedication, and an unmatched ability to bring out the best in his horses. Known for his calm demeanor, methodical approach, and a deep understanding of the sport's intricacies, Bill Mott has earned his place as one of the most successful and revered trainers in the history of thoroughbred racing. His journey to the pinnacle of the sport, his methods, and the recent success with his Derby-winning horse, Sovereignty, reflect the resilience and commitment of a true master trainer.

Early Days: From Humble Beginnings to Horse Racing's Bright Lights

Born in 1953 in the small town of Gallipolis, Ohio, Bill Mott's love for horses began at an early age. Raised on a farm, Mott had a natural connection with animals, and his passion for horses soon blossomed into a desire to become part of the racing world. Unlike many of his peers who came from prominent racing families, Mott was a self-made man. His start in the industry was not marked by privilege but by a deep passion for the sport. He began his career as an assistant to trainers before slowly carving out a niche for himself as a trainer in his own right.

In the early years, Mott's success didn't come easily. He faced numerous challenges as he learned the ropes of training horses, developing his methods, and establishing a reputation for being a dedicated, hardworking individual who understood the fine balance between a horse's physical and mental needs. But it didn't take long for the racing world to take notice of Mott's unique skills and unwavering commitment to his horses.

Mott's first breakthrough came in the 1980s, when he became a well-respected name in the industry. He began winning important races and attracting the attention of owners and breeders, who appreciated his ability to nurture horses and get them to peak performance. Throughout the 1990s and into the early 2000s, Mott's training operation grew, and he began to attract top-tier horses. His track record spoke for itself, with Mott's horses regularly finishing in the money at prestigious tracks such as Belmont Park, Saratoga, and Churchill Downs.

The Breakthrough: A First Kentucky Derby Win

While Bill Mott's career had already seen considerable success, the true validation of his methods and abilities came in 2019 when he won his first Kentucky Derby with the colt **Country House**. Country House's victory was a stunning upset, as the horse was not the favorite and had crossed the finish line in second place, only to be awarded the win after the disqualification of Maximum Security. The result was controversial, yet it was a historic moment for Mott, who had been trying for years to win the sport's most coveted prize.

Winning the Kentucky Derby is a milestone that every trainer aspires to achieve, and for Mott, it was the culmination of decades of hard work. The victory with Country House was a testament to Mott's patience and ability to bring out the best in a horse, even when the odds were stacked against him. Mott's win solidified his legacy as one of the greatest trainers of all time, and it also opened the door for new opportunities with owners and horses eager to work with a trainer who had proven himself on the grandest stage in the sport.

Despite the controversy surrounding Country House's Derby win, Mott's achievement was recognized by many as the result of his meticulous training methods. For Mott, training a Kentucky Derby winner wasn't about a fluke or sheer luck—it was about years of careful preparation, keen insight, and the ability to manage the mental and physical well being of a horse at the highest level. This approach would later be seen again in his training of Sovereignty, a horse that would go on to capture the hearts of racing fans and solidify Mott's legacy further.

The Methodology of a Master: Bill Mott's Training Philosophy

What sets Bill Mott apart from many other trainers in the racing world is his approach to training horses. While other trainers may focus on intensity and speed, Mott's training philosophy is based on a more balanced, patient approach. He believes in allowing each horse to develop at its own pace, understanding its strengths and weaknesses, and tailoring each training regimen to suit the individual horse's needs.

Mott is known for his calm and collected demeanor, which is mirrored in the way he handles his horses. He focuses on developing a close bond with each horse, establishing trust, and creating a relaxed training environment. Mott's training methods emphasize consistency, soundness, and longevity, all of which are vital for a horse's success, particularly in high-stakes races like the Kentucky Derby.

Mott is also a master of timing. He understands when to push his horses to their limits and when to give them rest, knowing that overexertion can lead to injury or burnout. His horses often run their best when it matters most—on the day of the race—thanks to his ability to judge their readiness and condition.

In addition to his physical training techniques, Mott is also highly focused on a horse's mental well-being. He knows that a horse's psychology can be just as important as its physical fitness, and he works to ensure that his horses are mentally prepared for the stress and pressure of racing. Whether it's a small local race or the grandeur of the Kentucky Derby, Mott ensures that his horses are in the right frame of mind to perform at their best.

Sovereignty: A Unique Challenge

While Mott's methods have worked with countless horses throughout his career, Sovereignty presented a unique challenge. Sovereignty, a young thoroughbred with immense talent, had the potential to become one of the greatest horses Mott had ever trained. However, Sovereignty was also a horse with a complex temperament and unique physical challenges that required careful handling and specialized training methods.

What made Sovereignty different from other horses was not just his physical abilities but the way Mott had to approach his training regimen. Sovereignty requires a careful balance of mental focus and physical preparation. Mott's skill as a trainer was tested as he navigated the challenges of working with a horse that needed both time and patience to reach his full potential.

The story of Sovereignty's rise in the racing world is a testament to Mott's expertise. It wasn't a quick fix or an overnight transformation. Instead, it was the result of months of careful planning, patience, and an unwavering belief in the horse's abilities. Sovereignty's victory in the Kentucky Derby marked a new chapter in Mott's career, a validation of his methods, and a reminder of why he remains one of the top trainers in the sport.

Legacy and Future: The Master Trainer's Impact

Bill Mott's career is not defined by a single race or victory. It is the sum of decades of dedication, hard work, and an unwavering commitment to the horses he trains. His methods have helped shape the careers of many top jockeys, and his influence can be seen in the success of the horses he's trained over the years.

Mott's legacy is one of integrity, patience, and excellence. He has proven time and time again that success in horse racing is not just about raw talent but about understanding the delicate balance between the horse's needs and the demands of the sport. His first Derby win with Country House, followed by the incredible success with Sovereignty, is a testament to his enduring greatness.

As Bill Mott continues to train horses and share his expertise with the next generation of racing professionals, his impact on the sport remains undeniable. His methods have changed the way trainers approach the sport, and his legacy will continue to inspire future generations of horse racing enthusiasts, trainers, and jockeys alike.

Team Sovereignty: The Heartbeat Behind the Champion

Behind every legendary horse, there is an army of dedicated individuals working tirelessly to ensure its success. While Sovereignty's name may be the one that echoes through racetracks, the true champions are the unsung heroes who made sure the horse was ready for every race. This is the story of the remarkable team that stood behind Sovereignty, working day in and day out to shape the horse into the phenomenon it became. From the grooms who provided the utmost care, to the exercise riders who helped sharpen his skills, and the veterinarians who ensured his health, each member of **Team Sovereignty** played an indispensable role in the champion's journey to the top.

The Grooms: The Guardians of Sovereignty's Well-being

The relationship between a groom and a racehorse is one of the most intimate and essential in the entire racing world. Grooms are often the first people a horse sees in the morning and the last they interact with at night. They are responsible for much more than just mucking out stalls or brushing coats. The grooms are the caretakers who create a safe, comfortable, and nurturing environment for the horse. In the case of Sovereignty, his grooms became more than caretakers—they were his guardians, ensuring that he felt secure and cared for at all times.

Every day, the grooms of Team Sovereignty would begin their day long before the sun rose. They'd start by ensuring that Sovereignty had everything he needed for the day ahead—fresh water, food, and a clean stall. They made sure his bedding was comfortable, which played a key role in his recovery after workouts and races. Horses like Sovereignty can be incredibly sensitive to their environment, and the grooms played a pivotal role in making sure he felt relaxed and calm. The routine the grooms followed helped instill a sense of stability in Sovereignty, allowing him to stay focused on the task at hand.

But the role of the groom goes far beyond just basic care. They were responsible for ensuring Sovereignty had the right balance of exercise and rest. Grooms monitored his behavior, always looking for subtle signs of discomfort, illness, or fatigue that might otherwise go unnoticed. They knew every little quirk about Sovereignty, from the way he moved to the sounds he made, and this attention to detail helped prevent injuries or illnesses before they could become problems. It's this kind of intimate knowledge that makes a difference at the highest levels of racing. Without the grooms, Sovereignty's journey to victory would have been much more difficult.

The Hotwalkers: The Unsung Heroes

In racing, the role of the hotwalker often goes unrecognized. These individuals are the ones who take the horse out for walks after each workout or race to help cool them down and relax their muscles. Hotwalkers help the horse recover from the physical exertion of a race or training session, walking them around the barn area at a slow pace while keeping a watchful eye on their condition.

For Sovereignty, the hotwalkers were crucial to his overall health and success. After each training session or race, the hotwalkers would ensure that Sovereignty's muscles didn't stiffen and that he cooled down properly. The recovery process was just as important as the training itself. With their steady hands and experience, the hotwalkers not only made sure Sovereignty felt physically good but also helped him remain calm and focused. These walks gave Sovereignty time to mentally unwind, reducing any stress or tension that might have built up during his strenuous activities.

Many times, hotwalkers become so attuned to the needs of their horses that they can tell when something is wrong long before others notice. The keen eye of a hotwalker can often detect subtle changes in gait or behavior that are indicative of potential issues. Sovereignty's hotwalkers were always alert, ensuring that any sign of discomfort or unease was quickly addressed. Their dedication to Sovereignty's post-workout care kept him healthy, strong, and ready for every challenge ahead.

The Exercise Riders: Shaping Sovereignty's Athleticism

The exercise riders are the athletes themselves. They ride Sovereignty every day during training, putting the horse through its paces and preparing him for the rigors of competition. Exercise riders are highly skilled individuals who need a deep understanding of horse behavior, fitness, and training techniques. They are the bridge between Sovereignty's raw natural talent and the finely tuned athlete he became. Every time an exercise rider swung into the saddle, they were shaping Sovereignty's future.

Exercise riders have an intricate job. They work closely with the trainer to create a daily training regimen tailored specifically to Sovereignty's needs. It's not just about speed—it's about timing, conditioning, and finesse. Exercise riders focus on improving Sovereignty's endurance, strength, and speed, but they also understand the importance of pacing and gradual progression. Their role requires both an intuitive feel for the horse's capabilities and a methodical understanding of what's necessary for race day.

They know how to challenge Sovereignty, pushing him to be his best without overexerting him. They also know when to back off, allowing the horse to rest and recover. Sovereignty's exercise riders played a major role in making sure that he was ready not just for one race but for a long and successful career. They were the ones who honed his talent and made sure he stayed sharp and fit, preparing him for the demands of each race he entered.

The Veterinarians: The Pillars of Sovereignty's Health

No matter how great a horse's natural talent may be, without proper veterinary care, that talent can quickly be undermined. This is why the veterinarians who cared for Sovereignty were integral to his success. Thoroughbred horses are incredibly powerful athletes, but like any athlete, they can suffer from injuries, ailments, or fatigue. The role of the veterinarian is to ensure that these horses remain healthy and strong, helping them recover from injuries and preventing future issues.

The veterinarians who treated Sovereignty worked behind the scenes, diagnosing and treating everything from minor injuries to more serious health conditions. They performed regular check-ups, monitored his diet and weight, and ensured that Sovereignty was physically prepared for each race. Their expertise was crucial in identifying potential issues before they became serious problems. They kept a close eye on Sovereignty's joints, tendons, and muscles, all of which are critical to a horse's racing ability.

One of the key roles of the veterinarian team was managing Sovereignty's recovery after workouts or races. Horses like Sovereignty push their bodies to the limit, and it's essential for the veterinarians to monitor their recovery process closely. From using therapies like cold water baths and massages to more advanced treatments like stem cell therapy or acupuncture, the veterinarians were always at the forefront of keeping Sovereignty in top condition.

A Cohesive Team: The Power of Collaboration

While each member of Team Sovereignty had their own specialized role, what truly made them a force was the way they worked together. Every person involved in Sovereignty's care understood that their role was part of a greater whole. The grooms, hotwalkers, exercise riders, and veterinarians didn't work in isolation—they were a collaborative unit, all focused on one common goal: the success and well-being of Sovereignty.

It was their teamwork that allowed Sovereignty to thrive and reach his full potential. Each member of the team brought their expertise, dedication, and passion to their work, and together, they made sure Sovereignty was always ready to face the next challenge. Sovereignty's success was not just a reflection of his natural ability but also the result of the unwavering support of those who cared for him behind the scenes.

The Legacy of Team Sovereignty

In the end, the story of Sovereignty's rise to greatness is not just about a horse's athleticism or the fame of his victories. It's about the people who supported him, nurtured him, and worked day in and day out to ensure he was in peak condition. Team Sovereignty may not have received the accolades or the recognition that Sovereignty himself did, but their role in his journey was just as important. They are the unsung heroes of racing, the ones who made sure that Sovereignty was always ready to give his best.

As Sovereignty's victories continue to be celebrated, it's essential to remember the individuals who worked tirelessly to make those victories possible. Their dedication, expertise, and passion for horses like Sovereignty are the foundation of every great racehorse's success. Team Sovereignty may have worked behind the scenes, but their impact was felt on every racetrack and in every victory lap. Without them, Sovereignty's story wouldn't have been nearly as remarkable. They are the heartbeat of the champion, and their contribution will forever be remembered in the annals of racing history.

Part III: The Path to the Derby

Every great champion has a journey. For Sovereignty, the road to the Derby wasn't just a string of races and wins—it was a story filled with determination, teamwork, patience, setbacks, and remarkable breakthroughs. Like all epic tales, it had highs and lows, moments of doubt and triumph. This chapter unfolds the inspiring journey of Sovereignty's rise from a promising colt to a leading contender for the most prestigious race in the country: the Derby.

A Star is Born: Sovereignty's Early Potential

From the moment Sovereignty stepped onto the training grounds, there was something different about him. He wasn't the biggest or flashiest colt, but he carried himself with an air of purpose. There was intensity in his eyes, a grace in his stride, and a fire in his spirit that caught the attention of every trainer, rider, and owner who saw him.

Though still young and raw, Sovereignty quickly showed signs of being a natural runner. His early workouts demonstrated speed, endurance, and a strong competitive spirit. But raw talent wasn't enough. To make it to the Derby, Sovereignty had to be shaped, tested, and proven against top-tier competition. That meant entering the world of graded stakes races—the essential stepping stones for Derby hopefuls.

Training Days: Shaping a Champion

The preparation for the Derby began long before Sovereignty entered any official race. It started in the quiet mornings at the training track. Each day, while the world was still asleep, Sovereignty and his team were hard at work. His exercise riders put him through tailored workouts designed to build stamina and sharpen his instincts. The grooms ensured he was well-fed, comfortable, and mentally calm. And his trainers closely observed every detail of his performance—how he moved, how he responded to commands, and how he recovered after each run.

One of the most important things in these early stages was building a strong bond between Sovereignty and his handlers. Trust between a horse and its team is crucial. Sovereignty needed to feel secure in his environment, understand his cues, and remain mentally focused. The team knew that it wasn't just about running fast—it was about learning to run smart.

The Maiden Victory: First Taste of Glory

Sovereignty's debut race—commonly known as a **maiden race**—was his first big test. Maiden races are designed for horses that have never won before, but they can be intense and competitive. Sovereignty didn't disappoint.

On race day, the stands were buzzing. Though he wasn't the favorite, whispers of Sovereignty's potential had started spreading. When the gates opened, he broke clean, held a solid position, and unleashed a strong final stretch run that left the crowd on their feet. He crossed the finish line first—a maiden no more.

That victory marked more than a win. It signaled to the racing world that Sovereignty was one to watch. It boosted his confidence and gave the team valuable insight into how he handled pressure and competition.

Climbing the Ranks: From Local Tracks to National Contender

With his maiden race behind him, Sovereignty began the climb through more competitive races. These included **allowance races**, **optional claimers**, and eventually, **graded stakes races**—the critical milestones on the path to the Derby.

Each race posed new challenges. Sovereignty had to adapt to different distances, track conditions, and racing styles. Some races had sloppy tracks from rain. Others featured fierce speedsters trying to outrun the field early. But time and again, Sovereignty proved his versatility. He could come from behind with a powerful kick or take the lead early and hold off challengers.

As he racked up wins and high placings, Sovereignty began earning points on the **Road to the Kentucky Derby**—a series of races that determine which horses qualify for the big event. His name began appearing in national rankings. Reporters wrote glowing articles. Fans started following his progress. But most importantly, his team never lost sight of what mattered: keeping him healthy, grounded, and ready.

A Setback in the Spotlight: Learning from Defeat

Every journey to greatness includes setbacks. For Sovereignty, that moment came in a key prep race: the Grade II Risen Star Stakes. The field was tough, featuring multiple Derby hopefuls. In the days leading up to the race, Sovereignty had been training well, but something felt slightly off. His team noticed he seemed a bit dull in his morning gallops, but there were no signs of injury.

Still, race day came. Sovereignty broke from the gate clean but didn't show his usual spark. He got boxed in early and couldn't find his rhythm. Though he finished a respectable fifth, it was a disappointment.

But the team didn't panic. They regrouped. A thorough vet check revealed a mild respiratory infection. He needed rest and treatment—but nothing career-threatening. They gave him time off, adjusted his nutrition, and focused on recovery.

That experience became a turning point. Not only did Sovereignty come back stronger, but it also taught the team the importance of listening to the horse. Success isn't just about pushing forward—it's knowing when to pull back.

The Breakthrough: Dominating the Rebel Stakes

After recovering, Sovereignty returned to the track with renewed energy. His next target was the **Rebel Stakes**, a Grade II Derby prep race held at Oaklawn Park. This was a crucial moment. A strong finish here would not only boost his point total but also restore confidence in his Derby dreams.

This time, Sovereignty delivered a jaw-dropping performance.

Breaking from the outside post, he settled mid-pack before unleashing a thrilling burst down the stretch. With powerful, sweeping strides, he surged past the leaders and crossed the wire first—ears pricked, barely winded. It wasn't just a win. It was a statement: Sovereignty was back, and he meant business.

The crowd erupted. Trainers from rival stables took notice. Overnight, Sovereignty became a top-five contender on the Derby leaderboard. The road ahead was clear.

Final Preparations: The Countdown to the Derby

With just weeks to go before the Kentucky Derby, the focus shifted to fine-tuning. Sovereignty's team entered him in one last prep race: the **Blue Grass Stakes**. Though the goal was not necessarily to win, they wanted a solid performance and a clean trip.

He finished a strong second, showing he could stay relaxed under pressure and handle the 1 1/8-mile distance. More importantly, he came out of the race healthy and eager— ready for the big stage.

As Derby Week approached, Sovereignty was shipped to Churchill Downs, where he began his final workouts. Under the twin spires, his presence was electric. Media followed his every move. Fans lined up to catch glimpses of the colt whose name had become a buzzword in racing circles.

But inside the barn, things remained calm and focused. His grooms kept to the routine. His exercise rider maintained the training pace. His trainer mapped out strategy. The message was clear: Stay humble, stay ready.

A Team Effort: Unity Behind the Scenes

The journey to the Derby is never a one-horse show. Sovereignty's path was paved by a team of passionate individuals who believed in him from day one. From the hotwalkers to the vets, everyone played a role. Their dedication, patience, and care made sure that Sovereignty not only reached the Derby but arrived as the best version of himself. They say it takes a village to raise a child. In horse racing, it takes a **team to raise a champion.**

Looking Ahead: Derby Dreams Within Reach

Now, as Sovereignty stood on the brink of history, the dream was closer than ever. The Kentucky Derby was no longer just a vision—it was reality. Everything he had done—every stride, every setback, every early morning gallop—had led to this moment. The path to the Derby was long, winding, and often unpredictable. But it was also beautiful. It showed the power of resilience, the value of teamwork, and the magic that happens when a horse like Sovereignty finds his stride. As the world waited to see what would happen on Derby Day, one thing was certain: Sovereignty had already earned his place among the greats—not just because of where he finished, but because of how he got there.

The Prep Races: Earning the Gate

Before a horse can run under the bright lights of the Kentucky Derby, before the garland of roses, before the thunderous cheers of over 150,000 fans, there's a road to travel. It's a long, gritty path paved with determination, grit, and skill. For the racehorse Sovereignty, this journey was defined by a crucial sequence of prep races—strategic stepping stones that shaped him into one of the top contenders in the world of horse racing.

This chapter dives deep into Sovereignty's path to qualification for the Derby—examining the key races, standout performances, point accumulation, and the teamwork that brought him to the most prestigious gate in American horse racing: Churchill Downs.

Why Prep Races Matter: More Than Just Warmups

In the world of horse racing, the Kentucky Derby isn't just another race—it's *the* race. But getting into the starting gate at Churchill Downs is no easy task. Only 20 horses make the cut, and they earn their place through the **"Road to the Kentucky Derby"**—a series of officially designated prep races across the United States and internationally.

These races serve two major purposes. First, they test each horse's ability, speed, and stamina against elite competition. Second, they award **points**, which are used to rank and qualify the top 20 horses eligible for the Derby.

For Sovereignty, each prep race was a critical chapter in his story. Every finish line he crossed got him one step closer to the Derby dream.

The Launchpad: Maiden Victory and First Glimpse of Potential

Sovereignty's journey started like most Derby hopefuls—with a **maiden special weight** race. This is a race for horses that have never won before, and it's often used to identify promising talent. From the moment he stepped onto the track, Sovereignty showed poise beyond his years.

In his debut, he broke smoothly from the gate, tracked the leaders patiently, and surged forward in the final furlong to grab a commanding win. It wasn't just the win that caught attention—it was the way he did it. Smooth. Controlled. Confidence.

The racing community started whispering: *This colt might be something special.*

Climbing the Ladder: The Allowance Route

After his maiden win, Sovereignty was entered into an **allowance race**, a step up in competition. Here, he faced more experienced runners and had to prove that his first victory wasn't just beginner's luck.

Again, he impressed. He settled mid-pack, displayed tactical speed, and pulled away in the stretch to secure a second straight win. Now, the whispers were louder.

Sovereignty was ready for prime time—the stakes races that would determine his Derby future.

Breaking Out: The Grade III Lecomte Stakes

The **Lecomte Stakes** at Fair Grounds marked Sovereignty's first big leap into the Derby prep race circuit. It was a Grade III event—competitive, demanding, and full of horses with similar dreams.

This was also the first race that awarded Derby qualification points (10-4-3-2-1 system). Sovereignty entered the race with growing expectations, and he delivered.

Though not the favorite, he broke alertly and settled just off the pace. As the field rounded the final turn, Sovereignty showed what set him apart—his incredible late kick. In the last eighth of a mile, he surged past the leaders to win by two lengths.

The win earned him **10 points** and placed him officially on the Derby radar.

Building Momentum: The Risen Star Stakes

Next on the agenda was the **Risen Star Stakes**, another major prep race at Fair Grounds, but this time with increased stakes—**50 points** to the winner.

This field was deeper. Horses like Stronghold, Eliminate, and Thunder Blast all had solid credentials. For the first time, Sovereignty would have to show if he could compete at the next level.

The race didn't start smoothly. A crowded field and inside post position left Sovereignty boxed in early. But patience paid off. His jockey, Junior Alvarado, found a seam on the far turn and gave Sovereignty the green light. What followed was magic.

Sovereignty unleashed a stunning burst of speed and won going away.

That win didn't just boost his point total—it made him a serious contender, with **60 total Derby points** now in the bank. He had one foot in the Churchill Downs starting gate.

A Test of Grit: The Louisiana Derby

The **Louisiana Derby**, a Grade II race with 100-40-30-20-10 points on the line, was the final big test before the Derby. This was a longer race—1 3/16 miles—and a true test of stamina. It was also Sovereignty's first encounter with a large field of well-rested and Derby-hungry challengers.

The team's strategy was simple: let him settle, conserve energy, and attack late.

But things didn't go perfectly. A slower pace up front meant the leaders didn't come back as expected. Sovereignty had to work harder, pushing wide in the final turn and rallying late. He didn't win, but he finished a strong **second**, earning **40 more points** and showing he could handle adversity and longer distances.

By now, Sovereignty had **100 Derby points**, more than enough to guarantee his spot in the top 20. But beyond the points, the race revealed something more important: this horse had heart. He could dig deep, even when the odds weren't in his favor.

Although Sovereignty had already qualified for the Derby, the team wanted one more prep—both for conditioning and confidence. They selected the **Blue Grass Stakes** at Keeneland, another major Grade I race with a big field and Derby implications.

This race wasn't about earning points—it was about sharpening tactics, gauging fitness, and keeping Sovereignty mentally fresh for the Derby.

He finished **third**, only a neck behind the winner. While not a victory, it was an ideal outcome. He ran strong, encountered traffic, and still pushed through. He came out of the race healthy and energized—ready for the ultimate challenge ahead.

The Points Breakdown: Road to the Derby Leaderboard

Sovereignty's prep race journey left him with a total of **140 points**, comfortably securing him a spot in the starting gate at Churchill Downs. His record heading into the Derby was:

- Maiden Win: No points, but built foundation
- Allowance Win: No points, but important experience
- Lecomte Stakes: 10 points (1st place)
- Risen Star Stakes: 50 points (1st place)
- Louisiana Derby: 40 points (2nd place)
- Blue Grass Stakes: 20 points (3rd place)
- **Total: 140 points**

That point total placed him **third overall** on the Derby leaderboard, behind only a couple of standout colts like Warline and Federal Rush. But many analysts agreed—Sovereignty had shown more consistency and resilience than any other horse in the field.

Behind the Numbers: What Made Sovereignty Different

While the prep races provided the structure, it was Sovereignty's *mindset* and *consistency* that set him apart. He wasn't the flashiest horse. He didn't always win by daylight. But what he did was compete—every time, against the best.

His performances showed he could handle different tracks, race styles, pace scenarios, and distances. He also developed a powerful late run that gave him a psychological edge. Competitors knew that if Sovereignty was anywhere near them in the final stretch, he was coming—and fast. And

Looking Ahead: From Prep to Prime Time

With the prep season behind him, Sovereignty arrived at Churchill Downs not just as a qualified horse, but as a real contender. His prep races had sharpened his body, strengthened his mind, and given his team a complete understanding of what made him tick.

He had checked all the boxes:

- Could he handle pressure?
- Could he race in large fields?
- Could he stretch out in distance?
- Could he bounce back from tough trips?

Now, the only question left was—*could he win the big one?*

Earning the Gate, One Stride at a Time

The journey to the Derby is not just about talent—it's about proving it, again and again, in the prep races that separate good horses from great ones. Sovereignty didn't take shortcuts. He faced challenges head-on, overcame adversity, and grew stronger with every step. By the time he arrived at Churchill Downs, he wasn't just a horse with points. He was a seasoned, battle-tested competitor with fire in his eyes and victory in his stride.

And that's how Sovereignty earned his place—not just in the gate, but in the hearts of racing fans everywhere.

Churchill in the Spring: The Electric Calm Before the Derby Storm

There's something magical about Louisville, Kentucky, in the spring. The air feels warmer. The skies open wide and blue. And the heartbeat of a city begins to rise—not because of a festival or a concert, but because of something far greater: **Derby Week at Churchill Downs**. It's a time when the city becomes the epicenter of the horse racing world. A place where tradition meets spectacle, and where the quiet hum of training grounds gives way to the roar of more than 150,000 fans on Derby Day.

But before the horses break from the gate, before the mint juleps are poured, before the anthem rings out, there is a week of preparation, tension, celebration, and pageantry. This is the story of **Churchill in the spring**—when the eyes of the world turn to Louisville, and the calm before the storm becomes a drama all its own.

Welcome to Derby Week: A City Awakens

As Derby Week begins, Louisville transforms. What might appear to be just another Southern city for most of the year suddenly glows with anticipation. Every street corner carries echoes of the past. From the airport banners welcoming visitors, to the decorated shop windows along Bardstown Road, the Kentucky Derby is *everywhere*.

Hotels are booked solid. Restaurants are bustling. Celebrities begin to arrive, and media crews set up their stations across the grounds of **Churchill Downs**. The entire city is buzzing—and yet, beneath that buzz lies a kind of focused tension. Because for trainers, jockeys, and owners, this is not a party. This is business. The biggest week of their careers.

The Morning Gallops: Training Under the Twin Spires

Each morning of Derby Week begins quietly—but not too quietly. By 5:30 a.m., before the sun fully rises, horses are already out on the track. These training sessions are some of the most crucial moments of the entire week. It's where the final touches are applied, the last-minute decisions are made, and strategies begin to crystallize.

Churchill Downs during training hours is a scene of discipline and poetry. Exercise riders steer powerful thoroughbreds through breezes and gallops. Trainers lean against rails with stopwatches, watching every stride, every flick of the ear, every drop of sweat. It's where the magic of race day is forged in silence.

For Derby contenders like **Sovereignty**, these early morning gallops aren't just workouts—they are **statements**. How a horse trains during Derby Week can shift betting odds, attract media attention, or raise eyebrows in rival camps. A sharp workout, a smooth gallop, or a show of eagerness can mean everything.

Media Frenzy: Cameras, Questions, and High Stakes

As the horses prepare, so does the media. More than 1,000 journalists, reporters, photographers, and broadcasters descend on Churchill Downs during Derby Week. It's not just about race analysis—it's about **stories**. The underdogs. The legends. The newcomers. The fairytales.

Every movement is tracked. Every word from a trainer or jockey becomes a headline. Interviews are scheduled around workouts. Horses like Sovereignty are no longer just athletes—they're celebrities.

For some horses, the attention is welcome. They strut in the paddock, pose at the rail, and dazzle under the flash of cameras. Others are more introverted, shielding themselves behind blinkers and handlers. But make no mistake—**every horse feels the tension** of the spotlight.

For the people behind the horses, it's a delicate balancing act. You have to entertain questions, give insight, and play the media game—while keeping your focus razor sharp. One misquote, one misunderstood comment, can trigger waves of speculation. But for a seasoned trainer or jockey, it's all part of the dance.

Backstretch Stories: Where Legends Are Born

Behind the racetrack, away from the grandstands and cameras, is a quieter world—the **backstretch**. This is where the heart of the Derby beats. Grooms clean stalls with care. Hotwalkers lead horses in lazy circles. Vets check legs and breathing. There's laughter, nerves, and a powerful sense of tradition.

The backstretch is home to the true heroes of the Derby—those whose names might not be in the program but whose work is essential. Many come from families who've been in the sport for generations. They know every inch of their horses. They watch for subtle signs—mood changes, eating habits, restlessness. Their bond with the horses runs deep.

During Derby Week, the backstretch becomes a kind of sacred space. Everyone knows the stakes. Everyone wants to be part of something unforgettable. And every so often, a horse emerges from that quiet corner and writes his name into history.

Betting Buzz: Millions on the Line

While horses train and journalists type, the betting windows at Churchill Downs start to come alive. The Derby is one of the most bet-on sporting events in America. In 2024 alone, **more than $180 million** was wagered on Derby Day. And much of that action starts during Derby Week.

Handicappers flood in, reading form guides and watching replays. Casual fans place bets based on names, colors, or gut feelings. Sharp bettors analyze post positions, track conditions, and pedigree charts. Everyone has an angle. Everyone wants their ticket to pay off.

For Sovereignty, the betting buzz was electric. After a strong prep campaign, he entered Derby Week as one of the top favorites. Each morning gallop, each breeze, each paddock appearance—everything influenced the odds. A great Tuesday workout could shift him from 6-1 to 4-1. A poor showing could cause concern.

The **morning line odds** posted by the Churchill Downs oddsmaker give the public a starting point, but by race time, the betting pool tells the real story. And during Derby Week, that story is always changing.

Fashion and Festivity: Style Meets Tradition

Beyond the racing action, Derby Week is also a fashion spectacle. From **Opening Night** to **Thurby** to **Oaks Day**, Louisville becomes a runway of southern style and bold expression.

Women wear elegant dresses with elaborate hats—some elegant, some outrageous. Men don suits in bright pastels, bow ties, and even seersucker. There's tradition here, but also room for flair. For locals and visitors alike, Derby Week is a time to dress up, celebrate, and be part of something iconic.

The **Kentucky Oaks**, held the day before the Derby, celebrates three-year-old fillies and draws a massive crowd of its own. Oaks Day is also dedicated to breast cancer awareness, with thousands of attendees wearing pink in solidarity. It's festive. It's emotional. And it's an essential part of the week's narrative.

The Calm Before the Roar

As the week progresses, the tension grows. By **Friday evening**, the horses are bedded down. The hay is fresh. The water buckets are full. The track is quiet. The stands are empty. And all across Louisville, there's a sense of stillness—**the calm before the storm**.

Trainers give final instructions. Jockeys rest, visualize, pray. Owners feel the weight of investment and hope. And horses? They know something big is coming. They sense it in the air. The energy. The expectation.

For Sovereignty and his team, Derby Eve is a time of reflection. They've done everything they can. The prep races, the workouts, the adjustments. Now, all that remains is the run.

Derby Day: The Storm Arrives

While Derby Day deserves its own chapter, it's important to understand that it doesn't happen in a vacuum. The magic of the Kentucky Derby is built during **Derby Week**—in the gallops, the interviews, the whispered predictions, the bright dresses, the early bets, the late-night strategy sessions.

Churchill Downs in the spring is not just a racetrack—it's a **stage**. A place where destinies are prepared and moments are carved into history.

And for every horse that enters the gate at 6:57 p.m. on the first Saturday in May, their journey through Derby Week is a crucial part of the story. It's where champions gather. It's where legends beg

The Field of Dreams: Derby 2025 and the Rivals That Stood in Sovereignty's Path

Every great champion faces a battlefield filled with worthy opponents, and the 2025 Kentucky Derby was no exception. As Sovereignty stood poised to chase immortality beneath the iconic Twin Spires of Churchill Downs, a cast of determined, high-caliber rivals surrounded him—each horse, each trainer, each jockey believing they too were born for greatness.

This wasn't just a race. It was **a dream forged by competition**, a collision of elite speed, heart, and preparation. Welcome to the **Field of Dreams**, where hope galloped on four legs, and where every contender brought a story, a threat, and a reason to believe they could wear the roses.

Sovereignty: The Horse to Beat

Let's set the scene.

Sovereignty, the colt who had conquered the prep trail with confidence, entered the 2025 Derby with a target on his back. His dominance in races like the Louisiana Derby and the Arkansas Derby earned him the favorite tag. He was smooth, tactical, powerful on the stretch, and had matured rapidly since his debut as a juvenile.

His morning line odds? **3-1**. He was the horse everyone feared, yet hoped to defeat. The question loomed: **Could**

anyone in the field rise up and challenge Sovereignty's reign?

Let's meet the warriors who tried.

1. Ironclad – The Relentless Closer

Odds:	**5-1**
Trainer:	Steve Asmussen
Jockey: Joel Rosario	

Ironclad was known as a **deep closer**—a horse who let the pace burn up front, then swooped in late like a thunderstorm. He came off a thrilling victory in the **Blue Grass Stakes**, where he made up 10 lengths in the final quarter-mile. His running style made him unpredictable but deadly in a fast-paced race.

His connections believed that if the Derby turned into a speed duel, Ironclad could capitalize. He was also proven over the 1 1/8-mile distance, and his pedigree screamed stamina. His late kick was breathtaking, but the challenge would be traffic and timing. Could he find room when it mattered?

2. Thunder Regiment – The Front-Running Fireball

Odds:	**6-1**
Trainer:	Bob Baffert
Jockey: John Velazquez	

When you hear "front-runner," you think of speed—and **Thunder Regiment** brought it in spades. A powerhouse out of the Santa Anita Derby, he blazed through fractions that would make even the boldest of horses blink. Trained by the legendary Baffert and ridden by Derby-winning jockey Velazquez, this colt had confidence and class.

Thunder Regiment's challenge was sustainability. Could he carry his speed over the grueling 1¼-mile Derby distance? Or would the ghosts of fast-paced flameouts haunt him in the final furlong? Still, nobody dared ignore a Baffert-trained bullet.

3. Crescent King – The Mystery from the Bayou

Odds: **10-1**
Trainer: Dallas   Stewart
Jockey: Florent Geroux

Crescent King didn't have the glitzy résumé of others, but he had heart—and a tendency to run his best races when overlooked. His second-place finish in the **Louisiana Derby**, just behind Sovereignty, turned heads. What made him dangerous was his versatility. He could press the pace or sit mid-pack and pounce.

Bettors loved his longshot potential. Analysts praised his work ethic. His final Derby work was sharp, and he seemed to relish the Churchill surface. Was he a sneaky spoiler? In Derby lore, these are the ones you don't see coming—until they're in front.

4. Mo Money Mo Speed – The Speed Merchant from New York

Odds: **12-1**

Trainer: Chad Brown

Jockey: Irad Ortiz Jr.

With a name that sparked curiosity and a stride that dazzled in New York preps, **Mo Money Mo Speed** was a fan favorite. He won the **Wood Memorial** with flair, zipping through the final furlong like a seasoned pro. Chad Brown's ability to get horses primed for the big day made him a serious contender.

But questions linger about his ability to handle a big field and the Churchill track. Was he just a regional hero or a national star waiting? With Ortiz aboard, he had tactical speed and championship instincts—but would they be enough?

5. Justice Rules – The Wise Guy Pick

Odds: **15-1**

Trainer: Brad Cox

Jockey: Luis Saez

Brad Cox had been knocking on the Derby door for years, and **Justice Rules** looked like his best shot yet. A colt with a grinding style and a big heart, he never ran a bad race. Second in the **Arkansas Derby** and third in the **Rebel Stakes**, he was always there—just one step behind the winner.

Analysts called him the "wise guy pick" because he didn't wow you—but he didn't disappoint either. Derby winners have come from this mold before. If the race got messy or the pace collapsed, Justice Rules could be picking up the pieces late.

6. Desert Phantom – The Wildcard

Odds:		**20-1**
Trainer:	Doug	O'Neill

Jockey: Mario Gutierrez

No one was quite sure what to make of **Desert Phantom**. Lightly raced but full of intrigue, he won the **Sunland Derby** in style and then trained like a beast leading up to Derby Week. His works were sharp, his gallops were strong, and insiders whispered that he was "sitting on a big one."

Gutierrez had guided two previous Derby winners (I'll Have Another, Nyquist), so he knew the road. Could this be the third? Desert Phantom was a wildcard—he could win it all or finish way back. That's what made him so fascinating.

7. Noble Flag – The Grey Colt with Grit

Odds:		**18-1**
Trainer:	Todd	Pletcher

Jockey: Tyler Gaffalione

Few horses looked as regal as **Noble Flag**, the striking grey who stormed onto the scene with a late-season surge. He ran a gritty second in the **Florida Derby**, holding off challengers late and showing real fight down the stretch.

While he didn't have the fanfare of some others, his consistency and powerful finishing run gave bettors reason to believe. And with Pletcher and Gaffalione teaming up, you knew he'd be ready. Could the grey be this year's surprise?

8. Tokyo Mirage – The International Intrigue

Odds:		**30-1**
Trainer:	Hidetaka	Mori
Jockey: Christophe Lemaire		

Every few years, the Derby field includes a **global challenger**, and in 2025, that horse was **Tokyo Mirage**, a Japanese-bred colt who made waves in the UAE Derby with a thunderous finish. Japanese horses had been making their mark on international racing, and fans wondered: could this be the year one takes the roses?

While Tokyo Mirage had never raced on American soil, his stamina, composure, and pedigree gave him a fighting chance. If he took to the dirt and stayed out of trouble, he could shock the world.

The Rivalry and the Race

Together, this field wasn't just competitive—it was **historic**. Eleven of the top 20 three-year-olds in North America stood shoulder to shoulder, plus international talent, elite trainers, and hungry jockeys. It was a melting pot of talent, ambition, and raw horsepower.

Each horse brought a different challenge to Sovereignty:

- **The Thunder Regiment** threatened to burn the race from the front.
- **Ironclad** could launch a furious rally if the pace collapsed.
- **Crescent King and Justice Rules** could lurk in perfect stalking position.
- **Tokyo Mirage** brought the mystery, and **Desert Phantom** brought the surprise.

There was **no room for error**, no easy leads, and no guarantee of glory. That's what made Derby 2025 a dream field. Everyone had a shot. And Sovereignty? He had to be perfect.

Only One Can Wear the Roses

In the end, the Kentucky Derby is more than just a race— it's a reckoning. A test of will, training, talent, and a little bit of luck. The 2025 edition was one of the deepest in memory, with a field filled not just with potential, but **with purpose**.

Sovereignty may have entered as the favorite, but the path was anything but smooth. The Field of Dreams was real. It was fast. It was fierce. And it was unforgettable.

Whoever won would join legends. Whoever lost would return hungrier. Because at Churchill Downs, every horse is a dream. But only one gets to live it out in a blanket of roses.

Part IV: The 151st Kentucky Derby – A Day When Legends Are Born

There are sporting events. And then there are **moments that stop time**, moments that grip the nation and capture hearts across the world. The **151st Kentucky Derby**, held on **May 3, 2025**, was exactly that—a celebration of speed, heart, history, and human emotion wrapped into two of the most thrilling minutes in sports.

This wasn't just a horse race. It was **a stage where dreams galloped**, where contenders turned into champions, and where history echoed through every thunderous hoofbeat. From the buzzing crowds dressed in vibrant hats and sharp suits to the fresh roses waiting to crown a victor, the 151st Kentucky Derby delivered everything fans hoped for—and more.

Let's dive into the race that stopped the nation and shook the racing world.

The Build-Up: A Nation Holds Its Breath

Long before the starting gates opened, Derby Day 2025 was already shaping up to be unforgettable. Months of anticipation built as prep races across the country narrowed down the field. From Florida to California, from Louisiana to New York, young three-year-old colts battled for their shot at racing immortality.

Every year, the Derby is more than a race—it's **an American tradition**, a cultural phenomenon watched by millions across the globe. Over 150,000 fans filled Churchill Downs in Louisville, Kentucky, with another 16 million watching live on TV and online. The scent of mint juleps, the roar of the crowd, and the beautiful hum of nervous excitement made Derby 151 feel electric.

In 2025, the field was stacked. It was **one of the deepest and most talented lineups in recent memory**, with speedsters, closers, wildcards, and a few international surprises thrown in. At the center of it all stood one horse— the favorite, **Sovereignty**—but the path to glory was anything but guaranteed.

Meet the Main Contenders

Let's take a quick look at the top contenders who lined up for Derby 151:

- **Sovereignty**: The favorite. He won the Louisiana Derby and Arkansas Derby with style. Strong, smooth, and seemingly unshakable, he came in at **3-1 odds**.
- **Ironclad**: The deep closer from Kentucky. Known for his late-charging finishes, he won the Blue Grass Stakes and was looking to mow them down in the final stretch.
- **Thunder Regiment**: The early speed. A Santa Anita Derby winner with fire in his legs and the legendary Bob Baffert in his corner.
- **Crescent King**: A bayou battler who came second to Sovereignty once and wanted revenge.

- **Justice Rules**: The grinder from Brad Cox's barn—always consistent, always game.
- **Tokyo Mirage**: The international mystery. Brought in from Japan, this colt had stunned in Dubai and was ready to shock the world.

All eyes were on this thrilling mix of horses, each carrying their own stories, dreams, and the hopes of trainers, jockeys, and owners.

The Day Begins: A Festival of Culture and Sport

By early Saturday morning, Churchill Downs had turned into a **festival of fashion, culture, and racing celebration**. Fans from around the world poured in dressed in traditional Derby fashion—big hats, bold colors, and stylish flair.

It wasn't just about the big race. The undercard was packed with Grade I races, rising stars, and future champions. But as the day unfolded, everyone kept glancing at the clock, knowing that **the moment of truth** would come just before 7 p.m. EST.

In the paddock, horses were groomed to perfection. Trainers gave final pep talks. Jockeys adjusted their silks, mounted their rides, and headed to the track.

Then the bugle sounded.

The 151st Run for the Roses: And They're Off!

As the starting gates clanged open and the horses surged forward, a wave of excitement swept over the crowd.

Thunder Regiment flew to the front, setting blazing early fractions. Just behind were Crescent King and Mo Money Mo Speed, keeping the leader honest. **Sovereignty** tucked in fourth, cruising comfortably, waiting for his moment. Meanwhile, **Ironclad** settled near the back—just where he liked it—biding his time for a late charge.

The pace was hot. The leaders hit the half-mile in 46 seconds flat, a testing tempo that would challenge any horse's stamina. As they rounded the far turn, the crowd began to rise. You could feel it—**the race was about to explode.**

The Final Stretch: Glory on the Line

Coming into the stretch, Thunder Regiment began to feel the heat. Mo Money Mo Speed surged, trying to take the lead, but then came the move everyone was waiting for.

Sovereignty, with a confident push from his jockey, swung to the outside and made his run.

With every stride, he cut into the lead. The crowd roared. Behind him, Ironclad was flying from the back—but had he left it too late?

In the final furlong, Sovereignty pulled even with Mo Money Mo Speed and pushed past. Thunder Regiment faded. Crescent King tried to re-engage. Ironclad was thundering down the center of the track.

But Sovereignty was gone.

With a powerful final burst, he pulled clear by a length and crossed the wire first. **Sovereignty had won the 151st Kentucky Derby!** The roar of the crowd was deafening. His name would be etched into history.

The Aftermath: A New Legend Is Born

Tears. Hugs. Smiles. Fireworks. It was a moment of triumph not just for Sovereignty, but for everyone who had believed in him. His trainer, a first-time Derby winner, wiped tears from his eyes. The jockey pumped his fist to the sky. The owners embraced in disbelief.

This wasn't just a win—it was **a statement**.

Sovereignty proved he had the heart of a champion. He faced pressure, battled off rivals, and finished strong under the brightest spotlight in racing. Fans already began whispering about a potential **Triple Crown** run.

The final results:

1. **Sovereignty** – Winner
2. **Ironclad** – A fast-finishing second
3. **Crescent King** – A game third
4. **Mo Money Mo Speed** – Showed guts in defeat
5. **Thunder Regiment** – Faded late but showed heart

Why the 151st Derby Mattered

This Derby wasn't just about racing. It was about **hope, courage, and belief**.

- For fans, it was a return to tradition and excitement in uncertain times.
- For the racing world, it showcased the **next generation of stars**, both equine and human.
- For history, it delivered another unforgettable chapter in the long story of the Kentucky Derby.

The race reminded us why this event matters. It's not just the mint juleps or the hats. It's not just the celebrities or the betting slips.

It's about watching greatness unfold—right before your eyes.

Looking Ahead: The Triple Crown Trail

Now, attention turns to the **Preakness Stakes** and **Belmont Stakes**. Can Sovereignty keep the dream alive? Only 13 horses in history have ever won the Triple Crown. Could he be the 14th?

The road ahead is tough. The Preakness is only two weeks away. The Belmont, with its grueling mile-and-a-half distance, waits after that. But Sovereignty showed he has the grit and fire of a true champion.

His name is now forever linked with greatness. And fans across the world will watch closely to see if this Derby hero can climb even higher.

Final Thoughts: A Race to Remember

The 151st Kentucky Derby wasn't just another chapter in a long book of racing history. It was **a classic**, a day when a brilliant horse seized his moment and reminded us why the Derby still matters after all these years.

Whether you watched from the stands, on your phone, or from your living room, you felt the magic. You felt the emotion. And you saw something special.

Sovereignty. A name now etched in roses.

As the sun set on Churchill Downs, one thing was certain: **we had just witnessed history.**

The Gates Open: A Moment-by-Moment Replay of the Race That Shook the World

The 151st Kentucky Derby had all the build-up of a championship fight. The excitement, the tension, the electricity in the air—it was all there. But when the time came, all of that buzz narrowed down to one sharp, focused moment. The world watched as twenty of the finest three-year-old colts on the planet prepared to make history.

This is the race as it happened. **From the second the horses were called to the gate to the final stride down the stretch,** every heartbeat and hoofbeat mattered. Let's relive the moments that made this Derby one of the most unforgettable races in recent memory.

The Walkover: Calm Before the Chaos

The crowd at Churchill Downs was at full volume, but in the paddock and tunnel, a deep hush settled over the teams. Grooms gave last-minute pats to sleek, muscled horses. Jockeys mounted up, adjusting goggles and whispering to their partners. These weren't just athletes—they were warriors stepping into the arena.

Sovereignty, the morning line favorite, looked cool and composed. His coat shone like polished chestnut under the Kentucky sun. Ironclad, the closer with the dramatic finishing kick, tossed his head and danced, already fired up. Thunder Regiment, a known front-runner, looked laser-focused. Each contender had a different strategy—but they were all heading to the same battlefield.

Post Parade: 20 Stars, One Stage

As the post parade began, the crowd erupted in cheers. Colorful silks sparkled as the horses pranced past the grandstand. The bugle call rang out—a crisp, ancient sound that always signals the start of something monumental.

Each horse was led into place, lined up in perfect formation. The starting gate, tall and green, loomed like a launchpad. The gates weren't just doors; they were the barrier between potential and history.

Tension gripped the crowd. Jockeys took deep breaths. Trainers looked on, eyes locked. Around the world, viewers leaned in.

The Loading Process: Seconds Felt Like Hours

Twenty horses. Twenty minds. Twenty hearts. The gate crew worked quickly and professionally, guiding each colt into its numbered stall. Some went in calmly. Others resisted. One or two pawed the ground nervously. Cameras zoomed in on Sovereignty's face—eyes sharp, ears pricked forward. He was ready.

At post position 10, Sovereignty stood like a statue. In stall 3, Thunder Regiment bounced in place, eager to bolt. Ironclad, way out in post 17, remained composed, waiting for the break.

Then, in the blink of an eye, the final horse loaded.

The red light flashed green.
The bell rang.
The gates opened.
And the Derby began.

The Break: Controlled Chaos

It was explosive. Controlled chaos in full gallop.

Thunder Regiment broke like a bullet from a gun, surging immediately to the front. His jockey hustled him out to establish position. Crescent King and Mo Money Mo Speed also broke sharply, angling toward the rail. From the middle of the pack, Sovereignty broke cleanly and smoothly—exactly how his team had practiced.

Further outside, Ironclad stumbled slightly at the break— not badly, but enough to fall behind early. He dropped to the rear, sticking to his late-run strategy.

As they charged toward the first turn, the field was tightly bunched. **Thunder Regiment led the way**, with Mo Money Mo Speed pressing him just off the hip. Crescent King held third. Sovereignty was fourth—saving ground, relaxed under a snug hold.

The First Turn: Establishing Position

The colts thundered through the first turn with a wall of noise behind them. The crowd—now at full volume—watched in awe as jockeys made split-second decisions. Some horses were boxed in. Others floated wide, risking extra distance.

Thunder Regiment continued to lead, setting a sharp pace. The quarter went in **23 seconds flat**—fast, but not suicidal. Mo Money Mo Speed was glued to him, applying subtle pressure.

Sovereignty, content in fourth, was galloping easily. His jockey never moved—just let the colt find his rhythm. Behind him, a pack of five horses battled for mid-pack position. Tokyo Mirage, the Japanese challenger, sat in sixth, looking comfortable.

Ironclad was still in last, but he was beginning to creep forward—just a whisper, but noticeable if you looked closely.

The Backstretch: The Race Within the Race

As they straightened out into the backstretch, the tempo intensified. This is where **the chess match** began. Some jockeys tried to slow the pace. Others urged their horses on, trying to gain better position before the far turn.

Thunder Regiment hit the half-mile in **46.4 seconds**. That was fast. Very fast. Mo Money Mo Speed continued to stalk him. Sovereignty sat chilly in third, still waiting. The trainer's instructions had been clear: *Don't move early. Save it for the stretch.*

Mid-pack, Justice Rules and Crescent King battled for position. The tension was mounting. Every eye in the stadium was glued to the track. Every heartbeat followed the rhythm of pounding hooves.

Ironclad, still far back, started to roll.

The Far Turn: The Fuse Is Lit

At the far turn, the real race began.

Mo Money Mo Speed moved first—launching an early challenge to Thunder Regiment. The two colts locked eyes, digging in as if the world had shrunk to just the two of them. For a moment, it looked like one of them might steal the Derby right then and there.

But then, like a hawk unfurling its wings, **Sovereignty began to move.**

His jockey angled him out. He swept three-wide, gliding like silk. The crowd saw it and gasped. You could feel the shift in energy.

Behind them, Ironclad swung six-wide and started flying—legs churning, eyes blazing.

As they reached the top of the stretch, Sovereignty pulled alongside the leaders. The sound from the grandstand was **deafening**.

The Final Stretch: Heart vs. History

This was it.

Thunder Regiment was spent. Mo Money Mo Speed was clinging to hope. But Sovereignty was surging, his legs devouring the ground.

The stretch was a battlefield. The Derby crown lay just ahead.

Sovereignty hit the front. The crowd erupted. Ironclad was still coming—faster than anyone—but the gap was wide.

For a breathless 12 seconds, the two favorites thundered toward the wire, chased by the rest. Crescent King rallied along the rail. Tokyo Mirage angled outside.

But Sovereignty had one more gear. With 100 yards to go, he found it.

He pulled away.

The Finish: Etched in Time

The finish line blurred beneath his hooves as Sovereignty crossed **first**, a full length ahead of Ironclad. The clock stopped at **2:01.88**—a fast, respectable time for the Derby.

The roar of the crowd was a wall of sound. The roses were ready. The legend was written.

Final order of finish:

1. **Sovereignty** – The new champion
2. **Ironclad** – A noble runner-up
3. **Crescent King** – A tenacious third
4. **Tokyo Mirage** – Proved he belonged
5. **Mo Money Mo Speed** – Gave it everything

The Afterglow: When the Dust Settles

As the horses slowed and returned to be unsaddled, the emotions poured out. Sovereignty's team hugged, cried, screamed. The jockey, holding back tears, tipped his helmet to the sky. The trainer collapsed into his assistant's arms. The owner beamed with joy.

It was a victory built on patience, preparation, and precision. Sovereignty didn't just win the Derby—**he conquered it**. The way he broke, settled, moved, and finished told a story of a horse who understood the moment.

As the garland of roses was draped over his shoulders, the sun dipped slightly. History had been made at Churchill Downs once again.

Why We Remember the Break

The Kentucky Derby is two minutes long, but the race is won—or lost—in those first few seconds after the gates open. That's when chaos reigns. That's when talent meets instinct. That's when hearts are tested.

"The Gates Open" is not just a moment. It's a beginning. It's a leap toward destiny.

And in 2025, Sovereignty took that leap—and never looked back.

The Stretch Run: Where Legends Are Made

There are moments in horse racing that feel like they freeze time. Moments where the noise of the crowd vanishes, where the pounding hooves become the only sound that matters, and where one rider, one horse, and one chance determine the destiny of dreams.

In the 151st Kentucky Derby, that moment came in the stretch run—a breathtaking finale where Sovereignty, with Junior Alvarado in the irons, seized greatness in a blaze of speed, courage, and perfect timing. This was more than just a race—it was a testament to preparation, trust, and a split-second decision that changed everything.

Let's rewind to the moment where all eyes locked on the final turn and the gates of destiny swung wide open.

Setting the Stage: The Race So Far

The early fractions of the race were hot and unforgiving. Thunder Regiment had set a wicked pace, and Mo Money Mo Speed was right there with him, pushing the tempo from the start. The first half-mile had gone in a sizzling 46.4 seconds—fast enough to break hearts and tire out leaders before they ever saw the finish line.

Sovereignty, by contrast, had played the waiting game. Alvarado never panicked. From the moment the gates flew open, he let his colt settle into a comfortable rhythm, tracking just off the pace, sitting in fourth for much of the way. He knew the race wouldn't be won in the first few furlongs—it would be won in the stretch, and Sovereignty had the tools to deliver.

Behind them, Ironclad was beginning to fly. Known for his devastating late kick, the crowd was murmuring as he circled horses and gained ground like a freight train on the outside. But all eyes were about to shift forward—to the front, where the final battle was about to erupt.

The Turn for Home: Eyes Up, Elbows In

As they approached the far turn, Alvarado made his move.

It wasn't sudden. It was smooth. He gave Sovereignty a subtle cue—just a shift of weight, a squeeze of his hands—and the colt responded like a coiled spring finally let loose.

Sovereignty edged off the rail and swept wide, positioning himself outside of Thunder Regiment and Mo Money Mo Speed, both of whom had begun to feel the toll of the early pace. It was a beautiful sight: a chestnut blur with pricked ears, eyes locked forward, and legs devouring ground with every stride.

In that moment, Alvarado didn't ask for everything. He didn't panic. He let Sovereignty build into his stride, stretching into the turn like a predator locking onto its prey. That's what made it brilliant—not just the move itself, but the patience behind it.

Other riders might have gone too soon. Some might have waited too long. Alvarado found the sweet spot. And when they straightened out into the Churchill Downs homestretch, Sovereignty was in full flight.

The Roar of the Crowd: Thunder in the Air

There are few sounds in sports as deafening and emotional as the Derby stretch run. When the horses turned for home and the field fanned across the track, 150,000 voices surged in unison, creating a roar that rattled the windows of the twin spires above.

Sovereignty, now with clear daylight ahead, struck the front with authority.

But it wasn't over.

Behind him, Ironclad was storming. The gray blur had gone widest of all and was coming with a vengeance. His stride was massive, powerful, terrifying. Every second counted. Every inch mattered.

To the inside, Crescent King was rallying. Tokyo Mirage found a seam and began to launch. But Sovereignty had opened up a lead—and he wasn't letting it go without a fight.

The Duel: Horse and Human in Harmony

Alvarado could feel it. He knew his colt was responding. But he also knew the Derby was never given—it had to be taken.

He dropped low in the saddle. He switched the whip to his right hand and gave Sovereignty a single, sharp tap. Not punishment. Not fear. Just focus. The message was clear: *This is our moment. Go.*

And Sovereignty *went*.

He dug in. You could see it in his body—shoulders rolling, hind legs pushing, heart driving. His ears pinned back, his neck stretched long. He wasn't running anymore. He was flying.

Alvarado's hands were still. He didn't ride with panic or desperation. He rode with trust. Sovereignty knew what to do—and the jockey was just there to guide him home.

It was horse and human in perfect sync. A dance in full motion, played out at 40 miles per hour down the world's most famous stretch of dirt.

The Challenge: Ironclad Closes In

But the Derby is never won without a fight.

Ironclad, with every muscle straining, was closing like a bullet. The margin shrank—five lengths, four, three, two. The announcer's voice cracked with excitement. The crowd was on its feet, shouting names, praying, willing their picks home.

For a heartbeat, it looked like Ironclad might get there.

But Sovereignty wasn't done.

He switched leads. Found another gear. And gave Alvarado everything he had left.

The final hundred yards were a test of grit. Sovereignty was tired, but not beaten. Ironclad was relentless, but still behind. The wire loomed ahead—red and white and final.

Alvarado looked up. One last look. He knew.

They had it.

The Finish: History in Every Stride

Sovereignty crossed the wire first.

One length. One perfect length ahead of Ironclad. A winning time of **2:01.58**.

The crowd exploded. Alvarado stood in the irons, fist in the air, overcome with joy. Behind them, the field galloped past in a blur, each horse a warrior, each rider a dreamer.

But only one pair stood in the winner's circle that day.

The Aftermath: Tears, Cheers, and Timelessness

As Sovereignty was led back to the winner's circle, cheers rained down like confetti. His flanks were heaving, his sides lathered with sweat, but his eyes sparkled. He knew he had done something special.

Alvarado dismounted and embraced the trainer. Reporters swarmed. Flashbulbs popped. Questions flew. But the answer was already on the track:

Timing. Trust. Heart.

That's what won the Derby.

Later, when asked about the move on the turn, Alvarado smiled and said:

"I knew what kind of horse I was on. I just needed to let him be great."

And he was great.

Why It Mattered: More Than Just a Race

The stretch run of the Kentucky Derby isn't just about speed. It's about **everything** that came before it—months of training, sleepless nights, miles traveled, challenges overcome. It's a test of stamina, strategy, and soul.

Sovereignty's win wasn't just a victory. It was a moment that **inspired**. For young fans watching at home. For breeders dreaming of their own Derby horse. For families who saved all year just to attend the race. For everyone who believes in comebacks, breakthroughs, and magic.

In that final eighth of a mile, the world stood still.

And when it started spinning again, there was a new name etched into history.

A Stretch Run for the Ages

The Kentucky Derby is a race of tradition and triumph, of legends and longshots. But at its core, it's about **heart**—the kind that beats in a rider's chest and in a horse's soul.

In the 151st running, that heart belonged to Sovereignty and Junior Alvarado. Together, they wrote a stretch run story that will be told for generations.

And for everyone who watched it unfold, whether in the grandstand or on a screen a thousand miles away, it was a reminder of what sport is all about:

The thrill of the chase.
The courage to believe.
And the glory of the stretch.

The Finish Line and the Roar: Where Glory Meets Thunder

There are moments in sports when time slows down. When every heartbeat echoes in your ears, and every second feels like a lifetime. In the world of horse racing, that moment is the final stretch—the chase to the finish line, the explosion of emotion, the roar of the crowd that feels like it could lift the grandstands off their foundation. And in the Kentucky Derby—the most iconic two minutes in sports—those final seconds are more than drama. They're destiny.

This is the story of *The Finish Line and the Roar*, the heart-pounding climax to the 151st Kentucky Derby. A tale of hooves pounding the dirt, jockeys driving with everything they've got, and a crowd erupting like a volcano when the race of a lifetime reached its breathtaking finale.

The Home Stretch: All Eyes on Sovereignty

As the horses came thundering down the final furlong, Sovereignty had a narrow lead. Junior Alvarado, crouched low and quiet in the saddle, was riding with laser focus. This wasn't just a race; it was a test of nerve, precision, and grit. His horse had taken command at just the right moment, and now it was about finishing the job.

The rail was a blur. The crowd was on fire. And behind Sovereignty, Ironclad was coming.

It was impossible to look away.

Ironclad, the brilliant gray colt with a reputation for late charges, was digging in—each stride more desperate, more determined than the last. His jockey was urging him, begging for more. The gap between the two horses shrank with every powerful push forward.

Sovereignty's chestnut coat shimmered with sweat and effort, his muscles stretching to their limits. The sound of his hooves hitting the dirt mixed with the rhythmic pounding of Ironclads approach. The finish line loomed— 50 yards, 40, then 30…

This was the Derby as it was meant to be: a battle not just of speed, but of soul.

A Roar Like No Other

At Churchill Downs, over 150,000 fans held their breath.

And then they *let go*.

As Sovereignty surged one last time, as Ironclad tried to snatch the dream away in the final strides, a roar erupted from the stands like nothing else in sports.

It wasn't polite applause. It wasn't a cheer.

It was thundering.

It was a wave of sound that started in the grandstand and rolled across the track like a hurricane. Fans screamed, cried, clutched each other in disbelief. They knew they were watching history.

People who had never met before grabbed each other like old friends. Bettors screamed their tickets into the sky. Children stood on tiptoes to catch a glimpse. Families leaned over railings, eyes wide and hearts pounding.

This is what makes the Derby magic. The crowd becomes one voice. One heart. One giant pulse pounding in unison with the hooves of champions.

The Final Stride: Destiny Delivered

As the finish line came into view, Sovereignty gave one last desperate push. Alvarado asked—and the colt answered with everything he had left.

Ironclad lunged with one final burst of speed.

But it was not enough.

With a margin of just one length—barely a breath—**Sovereignty crossed the finish line first**, his name forever etched in Kentucky Derby lore.

The clock stopped at **2:01.58**.

And just like that, the race was over—but the moment had only begun.

Silence After the Storm

For a split second, after the thunder of the crowd and the fury of the chase, there was a quiet. A holy, magical hush.

The horses continued galloping out, their riders pulling up. Alvarado eased back on the reins, stood tall, and let the moment wash over him. Sovereignty tossed his head as if he, too, knew he had just become immortal.

The silence was quickly broken by the eruption of emotions—jockeys embracing, trainers yelling in disbelief, and the roar returning again, louder than ever, as Sovereignty was confirmed as the **151st Kentucky Derby champion**.

The Walk of Honor

The winning colt, sweaty and proud, was led toward the winner's circle. Cameras flashed from every angle. Broadcasters shouted over the noise. Reporters scrambled to capture reactions.

But in the middle of the chaos, there was peace.

Sovereignty walked like a king, head high, eyes bright, as if he were soaking in the adoration. His saddlecloth, bright white with the iconic rose garland soon to be draped over him, fluttered in the breeze.

Alvarado, still on his back, tipped his helmet to the crowd. He looked around—at the sea of fans, at the cameras, at the people crying in joy or disbelief—and smiled.

This is what riders dream about. This is why they risk injury, train endlessly, and spend years waiting for their moment.

This was *the moment*.

In the Winner's Circle: History is Crowned

The Kentucky Derby winner's circle is hallowed ground. And when Sovereignty stepped inside, draped in the blanket of red roses, it was like watching a royal coronation.

Tears flowed freely. Trainers hugged each other, overwhelmed. The owners, dressed in Derby finery, wore expressions of disbelief and pride. Flashbulbs popped as the winner posed for the traditional photo—one that will hang in racing history forever.

For Sovereignty's team, it was the reward for years of hard work, heartbreak, and hope. The Derby is not given easily. It must be earned. And on this spring afternoon, they had earned it in the most thrilling way possible.

What the Derby Means

The Kentucky Derby is more than a race.

It's tradition. It's pageantry. It's a living, breathing story told once a year on the first Saturday in May.

It's silk colors flashing under sunlight. It's mint juleps, big hats, and southern charm. But most of all—it's *the roar*. That final thunderous sound that signals a new champion has been crowned.

And this year, that roar belonged to Sovereignty.

A Legacy Begins

Long after the horses cooled out, long after the crowds thinned and the track settled, one name echoed across Churchill Downs: Sovereignty.

He wasn't just a winner. He was a warrior.

He had held off one of the fastest closers in Derby history. He had risen to the challenge under the brightest spotlight in the sport. And he had done it all with grace, power, and the heart of a true champion.

For Alvarado, it was career-defining. For fans, it was unforgettable. For racing, it was a story that reminded everyone why this sport still captures imaginations after more than 150 years.

The Roar Lives On

Even now, as memories fade and new races approach, the sound of that final roar lingers. You can still feel it in the grandstands. You can still hear it when the gates open, when the horses round the turn, and when the stretch opens up in front of them.

It's a sound made by generations. A sound that honors the past and welcomes the future.

The roar is not just a cheer. It's a celebration. It's a salute. It's a thunderclap that says: "We were here. We saw this. We lived this."

And if you were lucky enough to be at Churchill Downs when Sovereignty crossed the finish line, you'll carry that sound with you forever.

Because in those final seconds, when history met heart, and the finish line turned into a memory, *The Roar* told the whole story.

Victory Lane: Where Dreams Wear Roses

There is a moment after the thunder of hooves dies down. After the race is run and the crowd's cheers echo into the sky. It's a moment not marked by the finish line, but by what comes *after* it—the celebration, the emotions, the tears, the hugs, the photos, and the unforgettable memories that are born in **Victory Lane**.

This is the heart of the Kentucky Derby's aftermath. A sacred space where winning is not just about speed—it's about sacrifice, teamwork, passion, and legacy. It's where the garland of roses is laid gently over a horse's shoulders, and the world watches as history is made in smiles, sobs, and snapshots.

Let's step into this magical moment and feel the rush of what it truly means to win the Kentucky Derby—not just for the horse, but for everyone behind it.

The Garland of Roses: A Crown of Glory

One of the most iconic symbols of the Kentucky Derby is the **garland of roses**—a stunning, hand-stitched blanket made of more than 400 red roses. This isn't just any flower arrangement; it is a royal robe of triumph.

As the winning horse walks into the winner's circle, sweating, breathing heavily, but proud, the garland is placed gently across its back. It shines in the sunlight, rich in red and lush with green ferns and baby's breath. The crowd erupts again. Flashbulbs go off. The moment becomes timeless.

For fans, it's a beautiful tradition. For the winning team, it's a dream come true.

The roses aren't just flowers. They're a symbol of everything that went into that win—the early mornings, the cold training days, the nerves, the setbacks, the prayers, and the belief that this horse could be the one.

Faces Behind the Finish: Emotions Run Wild

Victory Lane is more than a location. It's an emotion.

Tears flow freely—whether it's from the jockey, the trainer, the owners, or the grooms who've cared for the horse like family. These are real people, feeling real joy, sometimes for the very first time in their careers.

The   **Jockey**
The jockey is often the first to cry. After all, they were in the saddle, feeling every stride, holding onto every heartbeat. As they hop off the horse and walk toward the press, eyes glisten. There are no words that fully describe it. "We did it," they usually say, voice cracking. That's all that needs to be said.

The   **Trainer**
Trainers are like coaches and parents rolled into one. They've lived with the horse day and night. They know its habits, its fears, its strengths. When their horse wins the Derby, the emotions burst like a dam. Hugs, laughter, and the occasional disbelief ripple across their faces. It's not just a professional win—it's personal.

The   Owners

For owners, it's the culmination of risk and reward. Many have poured their savings, hearts, and hopes into one horse. To see their silks cross the finish line first is like winning the lottery—and even better, because this win carries legacy and emotion.

The   Grooms

The unsung heroes of every stable—the grooms—stand nearby, often overwhelmed. They've fed the horse, brushed it, walked it, slept near it. To see their "buddy" win the most important race in America is the ultimate thank you for their silent, behind-the-scenes work.

Microphones, Media, and Moments: The Press Frenzy

As soon as the roses are laid and the hugs are shared, **the media storm begins**.

Reporters rush forward. Cameras close in. Microphones pop up like mushrooms. Everyone wants a quote, a soundbite, a reaction. But in the chaos, you find some of the most honest and raw human moments.

The jockey stumbles through words, still trying to catch their breath. The trainer tries to stay composed but breaks down halfway through a sentence. The owner's voice trembles. And the horse? It stands calm, almost regal, as if it knows what it has done.

Social media explodes with photos and videos. The hashtag #KentuckyDerby trends worldwide. Fans from all over the globe begin sharing their joy, their reactions, and their love for the new champion.

In these moments, everyone connected to the horse becomes part of history. They are no longer just athletes or workers—they are *winners*, and the world sees them as such.

What the Win Truly Means: Beyond the Track

Winning the Kentucky Derby is about more than a trophy or a flower blanket. It's about **what that victory represents** for every member of the team.

For the Jockey – It might mean redemption after years of losses, or a career-defining achievement that forever cements their place in horse racing history. Some jockeys wait decades for a Derby win. Others win early but never again. Either way, it's unforgettable.

For the Trainer – It can mean validation. Every choice they made—the food, the workouts, the race strategy—was the right one. Trainers often face harsh criticism, so a win at Churchill Downs is the ultimate rebuttal.

For the Owners – It's a blend of pride and return on investment. Some owners are wealthy, yes—but many are small-time dreamers who took a chance. And when that chance leads to roses, it's a storybook ending.

For the Grooms and Stable Workers – It's a moment of recognition. The world finally sees the invisible work. The early mornings, the barn chores, the gentle care—it all led to glory.

For the Fans – Those who bet on the horse, or who simply fell in love with its story, feel a shared joy. The Derby connects strangers. At that moment, *everyone* feels like a winner.

Celebration Beyond the Finish Line

After the interviews, after the photos, after the garland and the speeches, comes the real party. Victory dinners, champagne, and laughter fill the night air.

The winning team celebrates not in flashy style, but in gratitude. They laugh, they cry, they look at each other and say, "Can you believe it?" It's a once-in-a-lifetime high.

Horses get pampered after their win. They're bathed, fed their favorite treats, and given time to rest. They're also visited by fans, photographers, and sometimes even celebrities who want to meet the newest Derby champion.

And everywhere the horse goes from now on, it will carry the title: **Kentucky Derby Winner**. That title follows it for life—whether it races again or retires to become a breeding legend.

Legacy Starts Here

Victory Lane isn't the end of a story—it's the beginning of a legacy.

From this moment, the horse's name is etched into Derby history, alongside legends like Secretariat, American Pharoah, and Rich Strike. Fans will remember where they were when they saw that horse cross the finish line. Children will grow up hearing about that race. And the people behind the horse will carry that pride forever.

Statues may be made. Paintings will be commissioned. Commemorative hats, mugs, and posters will flood Derby gift shops. The win becomes part of the Derby's ever-growing legend.

For the winning team, this moment becomes their *forever story*.

The Magic of Victory Lane

In a world of fast news and short attention spans, Victory Lane reminds us why we still watch. Why do we still dream? Why do we still cheer with all our hearts?

Because in that space, everything comes together—tradition, love, teamwork, and triumph. It's not just about who crossed the finish line first. It's about *how* they got there, *who* helped them along the way, and *what* it means now that they've arrived.

Victory Lane is not just a part of the Kentucky Derby. It *is* the soul of it.

It's where tears are honored, hard work is rewarded, and roses become more than flowers—they become a symbol of something unforgettable.

And for everyone who walks through Victory Lane, from the smallest groom to the grandest owner, one truth remains:

They didn't just win a race. They became a part of history.

Legacy in Motion: How Sovereignty's 2025 Kentucky Derby Victory Redefined Greatness

The Kentucky Derby has always been more than just a horse race. It's a living legend—a tradition that stretches back to 1875, when Aristides won the inaugural event at Churchill Downs. Each year, a new chapter is added to this storied history, and in 2025, that chapter was written by a bay colt named Sovereignty. His victory wasn't just a win; it was a moment that redefined what it means to be a champion.

A Triumph Against the Odds

On May 3, 2025, under gray skies and on a muddy track, Sovereignty defied expectations. Starting from the challenging 18th post position, he surged ahead in the final stretch, overtaking the favorite, Journalism, to clinch the 151st Kentucky Derby. The race was completed in 2:02.31, a testament to Sovereignty's speed and endurance. For trainer Bill Mott, this marked his second Derby win, and for jockey Junior Alvarado, it was a career-defining moment, especially poignant as he had recently returned from a shoulder injury. The victory also held special significance for Godolphin, the global racing operation owned by Sheikh Mohammed bin Rashid Al Maktoum, as it was their first Derby triumph after 13 attempts.

The Making of a Champion

Sovereignty's win was not just about the race day; it was the culmination of meticulous breeding, rigorous training, and unwavering belief. Thoroughbred champions like Sovereignty possess unique physical attributes—large hearts, immense lung capacity, and powerful legs—that set them apart. These traits, combined with dedicated care and training, create the perfect storm for greatness.

But beyond the physical, it's the intangible qualities—grit, determination, and the will to win—that truly define a champion. Sovereignty displayed all these in abundance, especially as he powered through the final stretch, leaving the competition behind.

A Legacy Beyond the Finish Line

Winning the Kentucky Derby is a dream for many, but for Sovereignty and his team, it was the beginning of a legacy. The victory resonated beyond the racetrack, inspiring fans and aspiring jockeys worldwide. It showcased the power of perseverance and the rewards of dedication.

For Godolphin, the win was a testament to their global racing vision and commitment to excellence. For Junior Alvarado, it was a personal triumph, a comeback story that will inspire many. And for Bill Mott, it was validation of his training philosophy and expertise.

Inspiring the Next Generation

Sovereignty's story serves as a beacon for the next generation of racers, trainers, and fans. It emphasizes that with the right mix of talent, hard work, and determination, greatness is achievable. As young jockeys mount their horses and trainers prepare their stables, they will look to Sovereignty's 2025 victory as a source of inspiration.

Moreover, the win has sparked renewed interest in horse racing, drawing in new fans and reminding the world of the sport's timeless allure.

A Moment Etched in History

As the garland of roses was draped over Sovereignty, and the crowd at Churchill Downs erupted in applause, it was clear that this was more than just a race—it was a defining moment in sports history. The 2025 Kentucky Derby will be remembered not just for the muddy track or the unexpected victory, but for the spirit of resilience and excellence that Sovereignty embodied.

In the annals of the Kentucky Derby, Sovereignty's name now stands alongside legends, a testament to what is possible when preparation meets opportunity. His legacy is in motion, inspiring countless others to chase their dreams, no matter the odds.

After the Roses: The Days Following the Derby and Their Impact on Racing Culture

The Kentucky Derby is one of the most iconic and celebrated sporting events in the world. Every year, the eyes of the racing world turn to Churchill Downs in Louisville, Kentucky, as thoroughbreds gallop toward the coveted garland of roses. The Derby is more than just a race; it's a spectacle that draws fans, celebrities, and press from all over the globe. But while the immediate excitement of Derby Day has passed, the days that follow are just as significant. The impact of the race lingers, and the aftermath of the Derby can affect not only the horses and their connections but also the broader world of racing culture.

The Aftermath of the Derby: The Public's Reception

As the dust settles and the cheers fade, the attention surrounding the Kentucky Derby shifts from the race itself to the aftermath. In the days following the Derby, the horse that won, along with its jockey, trainer, and owners, finds themselves at the center of the racing world's spotlight. The general public, media, and racing enthusiasts alike all flock to learn more about the horses and people involved, eager to celebrate the victory or analyze what went wrong in the case of a disappointing performance.

For the winner, the days after the Derby are often filled with excitement, media interviews, and appearances. Sovereignty's win in 2025, for example, was celebrated not only by the Godolphin team but also by fans who marveled at the horse's incredible journey from an underdog to a champion. People want to hear the stories behind the victory, learn about the horse's training regimen, and know what makes the jockey and trainer tick. The spotlight shifts to the relationships formed between horse and human, and fans start to view the champions as not just athletes, but heroes with compelling backstories.

However, the public's reception is not always as straightforward. While winners receive widespread adulation, the horses that don't win often face a quieter period. Fans, especially those who backed favorites, may feel disappointment or even frustration. But this is also the time when the narrative of perseverance, second chances, and future prospects becomes an important part of the racing community's conversation. For horses that didn't place, attention turns to what's next and whether they'll make a comeback in future races.

Media Coverage: The Spotlight After the Derby

The media plays a huge role in shaping the legacy of the Kentucky Derby. In the days following the race, news outlets ramp up their coverage, not only highlighting the winners but also diving deep into the race's dynamics, the performances of other contenders, and any behind-the-scenes drama. The press has a unique power in determining how the Derby is remembered—whether it's a thrilling triumph or a missed opportunity.

In the case of Sovereignty's victory, the media coverage was intense and focused on both the horse's performance and the story of Junior Alvarado, the jockey who rode Sovereignty to victory after returning from a shoulder injury. Press conferences, televised interviews, and features in major publications like *The New York Times*, *ESPN*, and *USA Today* helped magnify the significance of the win, propelling Sovereignty and Alvarado into the national consciousness.

Media outlets also scrutinize the other horses in the race, analyzing why favorites like Journalism didn't secure a win and what might have gone wrong in their performance. The media frenzy often sparks debates about the nature of the race itself, questioning whether the Derby is truly a test of the best horse or simply the most well-prepared. For fans and critics alike, the Derby is a topic of constant conversation long after the roses have been handed out.

Social media, too, amplifies the Derby's impact. Fans share their opinions, express their joys or disappointments, and offer insights on what the victory or loss means for the racing world. Memes, video clips, and posts flood the internet, contributing to the broader conversation around the race. In a digital age, the Derby is no longer confined to the stadium or television broadcasts; it's a global event that's discussed in real time by millions of people, keeping the conversation alive long after the race ends.

The Impact on Racing Culture

The days after the Kentucky Derby aren't just about a single race. The Derby's impact ripples through the entire racing culture, influencing everything from training practices to breeding decisions, to the culture of the sport itself. For the racing industry, a victory in the Derby can elevate the sport to new heights, drawing in new fans and increasing interest in racing as a whole.

One of the most significant ways the Derby impacts racing culture is through its role in shaping the future of thoroughbred breeding. The winner of the Derby becomes a prime candidate for breeding, as many owners and breeders seek to capitalize on the horse's newfound fame and success. Sovereignty's 2025 victory, for instance, would no doubt spark a surge in interest in the horse's bloodline. Breeders often place a premium on horses that have Derby-winning pedigree, seeing the race as a benchmark for greatness. This has long-lasting effects on the breeding industry, as the demand for offspring from winning horses grows exponentially.

Similarly, trainers and jockeys who perform well in the Derby often see an increase in their opportunities for big-money rides and more prominent horses in their stables. A trainer like Bill Mott, who secured his second Derby win in 2025, sees his reputation soar after such a major victory. For jockeys, like Junior Alvarado, a Derby win can significantly boost their career trajectory. Alvarado's victory in 2025 was not just about one race—it was a symbol of his resilience, determination, and skill, cementing his status as one of the sport's top jockeys. His win serves as a reminder that success in the Derby often opens doors to future triumphs, with winning jockeys often securing more lucrative rides in other prestigious races.

Beyond the immediate impacts on breeding and career prospects, the Derby's aftermath also shifts the way people view horse racing itself. In the wake of such a high-profile event, fans begin to see the sport not only as a race but as a celebration of tradition, athleticism, and human perseverance. The Kentucky Derby has the power to remind the public of the passion, skill, and dedication required to succeed in horse racing. It can inspire newcomers to learn more about the sport, attend races, or even become involved in ownership or training, which helps fuel the industry for years to come.

The Derby is also an important moment for horse racing's relationship with the broader public. Every year, millions of people watch the Derby, many of whom are not regular racing fans. For them, it's an opportunity to experience the thrill of the sport, the glamour of the event, and the excitement of the unknown. The aftermath of the Derby is crucial in maintaining that interest. It's the media coverage, the jockey interviews, and the continued celebration of the sport that helps keep these fans engaged, ensuring that the racing world doesn't fade into obscurity once the roses have been handed out.

A New Chapter in Racing History

As the aftermath of the Kentucky Derby unfolds, it's clear that the race does more than crown a champion—it shapes the future of the sport. The winners, their teams, and their connections become part of the rich history of the Derby, their names etched alongside legends of the past. But just as importantly, the race inspires a new generation of fans, breeders, trainers, and jockeys to dream big and strive for greatness.

In the days following Sovereignty's 2025 victory, fans and members of the racing community will continue to reflect on the performance, discussing every detail of the race and the impact it will have on the future. The ripple effects will continue to be felt, as the Kentucky Derby stands as a pinnacle of achievement in a sport that thrives on both tradition and the pursuit of excellence.

As the dust settles, the legacy of the Kentucky Derby and its aftermath will continue to influence horse racing culture for years to come. Whether it's through new fan engagement, increased interest in breeding, or the motivation it provides to future competitors, the Derby's impact is felt long after the final horse crosses the finish line. The days after the roses are just as significant as the race itself, reminding us that the true spirit of the Kentucky Derby lies in the moments that follow the victory.

The Triple Crown Trail: Can Sovereignty Claim the Preakness and Belmont?

The Kentucky Derby may be the race that stops the nation, but it's far from the final word in horse racing's most prestigious series—the Triple Crown. Winning the Derby is a monumental achievement, but the journey doesn't end there. In fact, it's only just begun. For horses like Sovereignty, who stormed to victory in the 2025 Kentucky Derby, the ultimate test is still ahead: can they claim the Preakness Stakes and the Belmont Stakes to secure the coveted Triple Crown? This trail is one of the hardest to navigate, but with a mix of talent, strategy, and a bit of luck, Sovereignty might just be the horse to conquer it.

The Triple Crown, which consists of the Kentucky Derby, Preakness Stakes, and Belmont Stakes, is one of the most difficult feats in the sport of horse racing. Fewer than 15 horses in the history of racing have claimed the prestigious title, and for good reason. The Preakness and Belmont are each unique challenges that test a horse's stamina, consistency, and ability to perform under pressure. After Sovereignty's impressive Derby win, the question on everyone's mind is: can he continue his dominance and take on the remaining two races?

The Road to the Triple Crown: The Preakness Stakes

The Preakness Stakes, the second leg of the Triple Crown, takes place two weeks after the Kentucky Derby at Pimlico Race Course in Baltimore, Maryland. It's often described as the "Middle Jewel" of the Triple Crown, and it serves as a crucial race for contenders looking to secure the title. The Preakness is a 1 3/16-mile race—slightly shorter than the Derby—yet it comes with its own set of challenges.

The unique aspect of the Preakness is its positioning so close to the Derby. Horses that have just raced in the grueling Kentucky Derby need to recover quickly, and the two-week turnaround is often a test of how well horses handle the quick pace of the Triple Crown. For Sovereignty, this tight schedule presents both an opportunity and a challenge. The Derby may have been a high-energy race, but if Sovereignty has the stamina and mental sharpness to recover quickly, he could make a strong showing in the Preakness.

Trainer Bill Mott, who helped guide Sovereignty to his Kentucky Derby victory, has the experience and knowledge to help his horse stay in top shape for the Preakness. Mott's strategy in the Derby showed his ability to adjust to the circumstances and let Sovereignty race with confidence. The key to success in the Preakness, though, will be whether Mott and his team can maintain Sovereignty's peak physical condition while giving him enough rest to ensure that he is still competitive.

It's also important to consider the competition. The Preakness usually sees a smaller field than the Derby, but that doesn't mean the race is any less competitive. In fact, the Preakness often draws some of the best horses from the Derby, as well as new challengers who didn't race in the Derby. Whether Sovereignty can hold his own against fresh challengers and Derby contenders alike will be one of the key storylines to follow.

The Final Stretch: The Belmont Stakes

If Sovereignty successfully takes the Preakness, he would then move on to the final leg of the Triple Crown—the Belmont Stakes. Held three weeks after the Preakness, the Belmont is the longest race of the series at 1 1/2 miles, testing a horse's endurance like no other. The Belmont Stakes is often referred to as the "Test of the Champion," and for good reason. Unlike the Kentucky Derby and

Preakness, the Belmont's length can take a toll on even the most seasoned horses, so Sovereignty's stamina will be key.

One of the challenges in the Belmont Stakes is the size of the track. Belmont Park is renowned for its sweeping turns and its long, straight stretch, making it a very different experience for horses compared to the narrower, shorter tracks of Churchill Downs and Pimlico. Sovereignty's ability to adjust to this unique configuration will determine whether he can succeed in the final leg. It's not just about physical speed but also mental fortitude, as the horse has to stay focused and pace itself over the course of the race.

The Belmont Stakes also has a way of separating horses that may have looked like Triple Crown threats after the Derby. The added distance and intensity of the race can reveal weaknesses or expose tiredness, and while Sovereignty's Derby win shows promise, it's impossible to predict how he will handle the rigors of the Belmont. As fans and experts alike know, the Belmont Stakes is often where true champions are made—or where dreams of the Triple Crown are dashed.

Expert Insights: What Needs to Happen for Sovereignty to Claim the Triple Crown?

Sovereignty's victory in the Kentucky Derby put him in an excellent position to continue onto the Preakness and Belmont, but achieving the Triple Crown requires more than just raw talent. In the weeks following his Derby win, racing analysts and experts have weighed in on what it will take for Sovereignty to complete the series.

Trainer and racing expert, D. Wayne Lukas, who has trained multiple Preakness and Belmont winners, believes Sovereignty has the right mix of speed and stamina to make it through the Triple Crown. "His Derby win was impressive, but the key now is how he recovers and whether he can stay fresh. The Preakness will be a big test—two weeks is a very short time to turn around from the Derby," says Lukas. "If he shows up fresh and focused, he has a real shot."

Fans and analysts alike are eager to see whether Sovereignty can handle the quick turnarounds between the races. The physical toll of the Derby is well-known, and while Sovereignty was impressive in his Derby performance, it's the mental aspect of racing that will truly make or break him in the Triple Crown races. Can he stay sharp, despite the pressure and expectations? Many are excited to see how he handles the Preakness, a race that will give them further insight into whether he has the legs for the Belmont.

Fans and Racing Culture: The Buzz Around Sovereignty

For fans of horse racing, the prospect of a Triple Crown winner is the ultimate dream. The Derby win was just the beginning, and now fans are anxiously awaiting each new chapter in Sovereignty's journey. On social media, the hype surrounding Sovereignty has been palpable, with fans rallying behind the horse and sharing their thoughts on whether he can go all the way.

"Sovereignty's Derby win was a thing of beauty. If he can keep up that pace in the Preakness, he could go all the way," says one Twitter user. "I've been a fan of Bill Mott's work for years, and I believe he has the experience to guide Sovereignty through the Triple Crown races."

Other fans have taken to online forums and racing websites to discuss the challenges Sovereignty will face in the coming weeks. There's no doubt that the Triple Crown is a massive feat, but the excitement and anticipation only make it all the more thrilling. With so much riding on Sovereignty's performances in the next races, fans have a lot to look forward to.

Looking Ahead: What Does the Triple Crown Mean for the Future of Sovereignty?

If Sovereignty is able to claim the Triple Crown, it will be a monumental achievement for his career and for the sport of horse racing. A Triple Crown victory cements a horse's place in history, and Sovereignty would forever be remembered as one of the few to complete the grueling challenge. It would also likely open new opportunities for the horse as a breeding prospect, further cementing his legacy in the world of thoroughbred racing.

Beyond the accolades, a Triple Crown win would have a lasting impact on the racing world. It would bring attention to the sport, rekindle interest in the history of the Triple

Crown, and inspire future generations of fans, breeders, and jockeys. Sovereignty's name could become synonymous with greatness, sparking debates for years to come over how his accomplishments compare to the likes of Secretariat, American Pharoah, and other legendary horses.

The Final Leg of the Journey

As Sovereignty's path from the Kentucky Derby to the Preakness and Belmont unfolds, the excitement around his potential to claim the Triple Crown continues to build. The journey ahead is tough, with each race testing a horse's limits and character in different ways. For Sovereignty, it's not just about raw ability but also mental toughness and the support of an experienced team behind him.

Whether or not Sovereignty can claim the Triple Crown remains to be seen, but one thing is certain: his journey has captured the hearts of fans and experts alike. The Triple Crown Trail is a path few horses have successfully navigated, but if Sovereignty can conquer the Preakness and Belmont, he will join a rare group of champions whose legacies are forever etched in the history of racing.

The Mark They Left: How the 2025 Derby Redefined Careers

In the world of horse racing, the Kentucky Derby is more than just a race—it's a defining moment in the careers of horses, jockeys, trainers, and even owners. The 2025 Derby, held at Churchill Downs on the first Saturday in May, was one such event that left an indelible mark on the sport, forever changing the trajectories of those involved. It wasn't just a race that ended with a victor; it was a race that launched careers, reaffirmed legacies, and added a new chapter to the rich history of thoroughbred racing. This year, the Kentucky Derby wasn't just about Sovereignty's impressive victory—it was about the personal milestones reached by the people behind the scenes and the redefined place of racing's legends in the sport's annals. In many ways, the 2025 Derby didn't just give us a winner; it gave us a renewed understanding of what it means to succeed in this sport.

Alvarado's First Win: The Moment That Made a Jockey's Career

For jockey Antonio Alvarado, his victory aboard Sovereignty in the 2025 Kentucky Derby was a moment years in the making. Alvarado, known for his quiet determination and consistent performances in smaller stakes races, had always been a promising rider but had yet to capture a win in racing's most prestigious event. For many, the Kentucky Derby represents the pinnacle of a jockey's career. The pressure of riding in front of thousands of passionate fans, alongside some of the best riders in the world, is immense. But for Alvarado, it was a dream fulfilled.

The 2025 Derby was his first opportunity to ride in the race, and it was a chance he seized with both hands. The bond between Alvarado and Sovereignty was immediate, and it showed in the way they executed their strategy. They had a perfect run, with Alvarado's experience in navigating the tight turns of Churchill Downs' track shining through. The way he guided Sovereignty through the field, making critical moves at just the right moments, was a textbook display of what it takes to win the Derby.

After crossing the finish line, Alvarado's joy was palpable. For him, the victory was not only a personal achievement but a statement to the racing world. "I've been working toward this moment my whole life," he said after the race. "Winning the Derby means everything to me. It's something every jockey dreams of, and to have it come true today with Sovereignty is just beyond words."

Alvarado's first win at the Derby was not just a career milestone—it was a moment that redefined his reputation. Jockeys often have to work their way up the ranks, but after his triumph, Alvarado's place among the elite of the sport was assured. He went from being a talented rider with potential to a household name. Moving forward, this victory would serve as the foundation upon which his career would be built, and it would only add to the mounting respect he has earned within the racing community.

Mott's Second Crown: A Trainer's Legacy Reaffirmed

For trainer Bill Mott, the 2025 Kentucky Derby victory was a monumental achievement of its own. Mott, a revered figure in racing, had already cemented his legacy with victories in major races, including a triumph in the Derby in 2011 with Animal Kingdom. Yet, winning the Derby again in 2025 with Sovereignty didn't just add another notch to his belt—it reaffirmed his mastery of training thoroughbreds at the highest level.

Mott's training style has always been known for its meticulous attention to detail and his ability to bring horses to peak performance when it matters most. With Sovereignty, Mott once again demonstrated his unparalleled ability to manage the preparation of a horse for one of the most demanding races in the world. From the initial stages of Sovereignty's training to the moment he crossed the finish line first in the Derby, Mott's strategy had been flawless.

The victory was particularly sweet for Mott because it showcased his ability to adapt his training methods to the unique needs of each horse. While Animal Kingdom was a versatile and resilient horse in his own right, Sovereignty had his own distinct characteristics. Sovereignty wasn't just a fast horse—he was one with incredible stamina and an almost calm demeanor in the midst of intense competition. Mott knew exactly how to harness those strengths and put Sovereignty in the best position to succeed.

For Mott, the 2025 Derby win was also a testament to the decades of dedication he has poured into the sport. To win the Derby twice, in two different decades, solidifies Mott as one of the greatest trainers in racing history. "You never take winning the Derby for granted. It's always special," Mott said in the aftermath of the victory. "This one feels especially good because it's with a horse like Sovereignty, who has so much talent and heart. It's an honor to be part of his journey."

Mott's second Kentucky Derby win strengthened his already legendary reputation and gave him even more credibility in the racing world. It was proof that, after years of success, he still had what it takes to bring home the most coveted prize in the sport. As the trainer of Sovereignty, Mott's legacy was further etched into the history of the Kentucky Derby, reaffirming his place among the greatest to ever lead a horse to victory.

Sovereignty's Place in Racing Lore: A New Champion Emerges

While Alvarado's and Mott's victories were pivotal, perhaps the most significant takeaway from the 2025 Kentucky Derby was Sovereignty's own place in racing lore. Sovereignty's victory marked him as a new champion—a horse who had all the qualities necessary to go down in history as one of the sport's greats.

Sovereignty was no ordinary Derby winner. From the moment he began his career, his pedigree was clear—he had the potential to be a standout in the world of thoroughbred racing. His sire, Empire's Reign, was known for producing talented horses, and Sovereignty carried that legacy forward. His dam, a former stakes winner herself, had given him a solid foundation. But it was Sovereignty's performance in the 2025 Derby that truly revealed the depth of his talent. He handled the stress of the race with grace, outrunning some of the most promising contenders and displaying remarkable stamina in the final stretch.

What made Sovereignty even more compelling was his personality and his resilience. He wasn't a flashy horse, but he had the heart of a champion. Whether it was his ability to maintain a steady pace throughout the race or his unshakable focus in the final stretch, Sovereignty proved that he wasn't just another winner—he was a horse built for greatness.

Sovereignty's victory in the 2025 Derby secured him a spot in the history books, but his journey didn't stop there. The Triple Crown remained a tantalizing goal. The racing world will be watching his every move in the upcoming Preakness and Belmont Stakes, eager to see if he can complete the series and claim the ultimate title in thoroughbred racing.

The Impact on Racing Culture: How the 2025 Derby Redefined Careers

The 2025 Kentucky Derby wasn't just about the people and horses involved; it had a lasting impact on the culture of racing itself. In a sport that thrives on tradition, the Derby often serves as a touchstone for the future, as it blends history with the promise of what's to come. The performances of Alvarado, Mott, and Sovereignty in 2025 proved that while racing is steeped in tradition, it is also a sport where new names can rise, and new stories can unfold.

For Alvarado, the Derby was a breakthrough moment, reminding the racing community that there's always room for fresh talent. For Mott, it was a reaffirmation of his legendary status, showing that experience and adaptability are crucial in maintaining success over the years. For Sovereignty, the Derby win was a defining moment that announced his arrival as a true champion. The 2025 Derby was a race where new legends were born and where careers were transformed.

In many ways, the 2025 Kentucky Derby redefined the racing landscape. It reminded the world that success in horse racing isn't just about winning; it's about the stories of dedication, passion, and perseverance that come with each victory. It's about the jockey who works tirelessly to improve, the trainer who crafts the perfect plan, and the horse who defies expectations to leave his mark on history.

As the years go by and future generations of racing fans reflect on the great moments in the sport, the 2025 Derby will stand as one of those pivotal moments. It will be remembered as the day Alvarado, Mott, and Sovereignty each carved out their own place in racing history, leaving a mark that will never be forgotten.

Epilogue – More Than a Race: The Legacy of Champions and the Timeless Allure of the Kentucky Derby

The Kentucky Derby is far more than a race; it is a celebration of history, a symbol of tradition, and a reminder of the timeless spirit of competition. Held every first Saturday in May at the iconic Churchill Downs in Louisville, Kentucky, this event stands as the epitome of horse racing in the United States and around the world. It is an event that draws millions of spectators, from casual fans to passionate racing enthusiasts, all eager to witness the spectacle that has become known as "The Greatest Two Minutes in Sports."

But what is it about the Kentucky Derby that continues to captivate hearts and minds, year after year? Why does it inspire such devotion, not just in the people who watch it, but in those who participate in it—jockeys, trainers, owners, and, of course, the horses themselves? The answer is deeper than the thrill of a race; it lies in the very essence of what makes the Derby more than just a contest of speed.

The Beauty of Tradition

One of the most powerful aspects of the Kentucky Derby is its deep-rooted connection to tradition. The race, first run in 1875, has a rich history that spans over 140 years. This long legacy carries with it a sense of pride and continuity, and for those involved in the sport, the Derby is a culmination of years of hard work, training, and sacrifice. For the horses, their journey to the Derby begins long before they step onto the track—they are carefully bred, trained, and conditioned to compete at the highest level.

The Kentucky Derby has always been more than just an athletic event; it is a symbol of what happens when dedication and passion come together. From the iconic Mint Julep served in the stands to the famous floral garlands draped over the winning horse, every detail of the event is steeped in time-honored customs. The race's most famous tradition, the singing of "My Old Kentucky Home," is a poignant reminder of the deep cultural significance of the Derby, connecting participants and fans alike to the heart of Kentucky's heritage.

This commitment to tradition is what keeps the Kentucky Derby relevant year after year. Each year, there are new horses, new jockeys, and new stories, but the essence of the event remains the same. It is an annual celebration of excellence, where the brightest stars of the thoroughbred racing world come together to create history.

A Celebration of Champions

At the heart of the Kentucky Derby lies the celebration of champions. The winner of the race becomes an instant legend, etching their name into the history books alongside the greatest horses and jockeys the sport has ever known. Horses like Secretariat, Man o' War, and American Pharoah are immortalized as icons of the sport, their victories at the Derby serving as defining moments in their careers.

But while the champions of the Kentucky Derby are immortalized in the annals of racing history, it's the legacy of those who come in second, third, or fourth that adds a layer of complexity to the race. The Derby is a unique event because it's not just about the horse that crosses the finish line first. It's about the entire journey—the years of hard work and training that lead to that moment. It's about the horses that come so close, but don't quite make it, and the jockeys who give their all but fall short of the victory. The Kentucky Derby celebrates them all, and it is this inclusivity that makes the event resonate so deeply.

The race itself is often unpredictable—no one can ever truly know who will come out on top. Every horse in the race has a chance to make history. And while there may only be one winner, the Kentucky Derby brings attention to every horse and jockey who participates, celebrating the spirit of competition and the dedication that goes into becoming a contender.

The Connection Between Humans and Horses

What sets horse racing apart from many other sports is the unique bond between human and animal. In no other sport do athletes rely so heavily on one another. The bond between a jockey and their horse is one of mutual trust, understanding, and respect. In the Kentucky Derby, every horse has been trained to perform at the highest level, and every jockey has spent countless hours building a relationship with their mount to ensure they're in perfect sync during the race.

For the horses, it's not just about running fast—it's about having the heart and the will to perform under pressure. The connection between jockey and horse goes beyond training and preparation. It is a deep, intuitive bond that can only be forged through experience and mutual respect. Jockeys often speak of the special relationship they have with their Derby mounts, describing how they come to understand their horse's temperament, how they respond to subtle cues, and how they work together as a team.

This human-animal partnership is something that is celebrated every year at the Kentucky Derby. It is not just about the speed or the beauty of the horses; it's about the extraordinary collaboration between the jockeys and their mounts. And it is this partnership that allows both man and beast to achieve greatness together.

The Universal Appeal of the Derby

While the Kentucky Derby is a quintessentially American event, its appeal extends far beyond the borders of the United States. People from all over the world tune in to watch the race, and its impact on global culture cannot be overstated. The Derby transcends cultural boundaries, attracting fans from all walks of life. It is a gathering of people united by their love of racing, of tradition, and of the sheer thrill of competition.

For those who attend the race in person, the Kentucky Derby is an experience unlike any other. The atmosphere at Churchill Downs is electric, filled with excitement, anticipation, and celebration. People come dressed to the nines, donning elaborate hats and seersucker suits, adding a sense of glamour and elegance to the event. For many, attending the Kentucky Derby is a once-in-a-lifetime experience, and it's a tradition passed down from generation to generation. It's a social event, a chance to dress up and enjoy the thrill of watching the greatest horses in the world compete.

For others, the Kentucky Derby is a chance to experience the magic of the race from home. It's a tradition shared with family and friends, where people gather to watch the race, place bets, and cheer on their favorite horses. It's an event that brings people together, whether they are at the track or watching from the comfort of their living rooms.

The Enduring Legacy of the Kentucky Derby

The Kentucky Derby is more than just a race; it is an enduring symbol of excellence, tradition, and the power of the human spirit. For the horses, jockeys, and trainers who participate, it is the culmination of a lifetime of work, sacrifice, and dedication. And for the fans who watch, it is a reminder of the beauty of sport and the deep, unbreakable bond between man and animal.

As long as the Kentucky Derby continues, it will remain a testament to the lasting impact of champions, to the legacy of those who strive to be great, and to the power of competition to bring people together. Every year, a new winner is crowned, but the spirit of the race remains unchanged. It is a timeless celebration of what it means to be part of something greater than oneself, and it continues to captivate the hearts and minds of fans around the world.

The Kentucky Derby is more than just a race—it is a living, breathing legacy. And as the years go by, it will continue to inspire new generations of fans and athletes, each hoping to carve their own place in history.

Conclusion

The Kentucky Derby is not just a race; it is an institution, a celebration of tradition, culture, and the relentless pursuit of greatness. From its humble beginnings in 1875 to its status as "The Greatest Two Minutes in Sports," the Derby has captivated hearts and minds across generations, drawing together people from all walks of life. Whether it's the iconic Mint Juleps, the dazzling fashion, or the powerful moments of triumph and heartbreak on the racetrack, the Derby represents more than just competition—it's a reflection of the human spirit, the bond between jockey and horse, and the timeless allure of the sport.

Throughout this book, we've explored the profound significance of the Kentucky Derby, not only as a premier sporting event but as a symbol of excellence, perseverance, and tradition. From the champions that have etched their names into the history books to the unsung heroes who come close but don't win, each participant contributes to the Derby's rich legacy. It's a race where every contender matters, and every story adds to the broader narrative of what makes this event so special.

In essence, the Kentucky Derby stands as a testament to the power of competition, the beauty of tradition, and the profound connections that sports can forge. It is a celebration of the pursuit of perfection, where humans and horses come together to achieve greatness. The Derby's enduring legacy is not just in the victories, but in the stories it creates—stories of dedication, of overcoming obstacles, and of shared experiences that unite us all.

As we look ahead, the Kentucky Derby will continue to inspire future generations of fans, trainers, jockeys, and horses to chase the dream of victory and, in doing so, become part of this ever-evolving tradition. It will remain an event that transcends time, a moment of collective joy and anticipation, where the thrill of competition meets the beauty of history. The Derby is more than just a race—it is a legacy, one that will continue to shine brightly for years to come.

Made in the USA
Las Vegas, NV
12 May 2025